COMPILED AND WITH
AN INTRODUCTION BY

Stuart Y. Silverstein

SCRIBNER
NEW YORK LONDON TORONTO SYDNEY

Not Much Fun

The Lost Poems of
DOROTHY PARKER

SCRIBNER

A Division of Simon & Schuster, Inc.

1230 Avenue of the Americas

New York, NY 10020

This book is a work of fiction. Names, characters, places,
and incidents either are products of the author's imagination or
are used fictitiously. Any resemblance to actual events or locales
or persons, living or dead, is entirely coincidental.

This Scribner trade paperback edition October 2009

SCRIBNER and design are trademarks of The Gale Group, Inc., used under
license by Simon & Schuster, Inc., the publisher of this work.

For information about special discounts for bulk purchases, please
contact Simon & Schuster Special Sales at 1-866-506-1949 or
business@simonandschuster.com.

The Simon & Schuster Speakers Bureau can bring authors to your
live event. For more information or to book an event contact the
Simon & Schuster Speakers Bureau at 1-866-248-3049 or
visit our website at www.simonspeakers.com.

Manufactured in the United States of America

3 5 7 9 10 8 6 4 2

Library of Congress Control Number: 96016287

ISBN 978-1-4391-4317-9
ISBN 978-1-4391-3105-3 (ebook)

Owing to limitations of space, text permissions appear on page 272.

Contents

The "Hate Verses"

Introduction

The literary gadfly Alexander Woollcott was uncharacteristically benevolent as he declared his admiration for Dorothy Parker in the short (eleven-page) but influential profile that appeared in his best-selling 1934 essay collection, *While Rome Burns*. "Our Mrs. Parker" was "a little and extraordinarily pretty woman." Her work was "pure gold" that would be celebrated by future generations. She possessed "the gentlest, most disarming demeanor" while she wielded a verbal "dirk which knows no brother and mighty few sisters." Perhaps she was notorious for stalking human prey, but she loved other animals with a visceral passion. She was "so odd a blend of Little Nell and Lady Macbeth," whose weapon was "not so much the familiar hand of steel in a velvet glove as a lacy sleeve with a bottle of vitriol concealed in its folds."

In the course of the profile Woollcott catalogued many of the wisecracks, retorts, and assorted quips that had been attributed to Dorothy over the preceding fifteen years.[1] But if Doro-

---

1. It is dangerous to attribute particular anecdotes or witticisms to Dottie. Many are at least partly apocryphal, or are known in several conflicting accounts (each with its own version of parties and dialogue), but conversation is ephemeral, and it is often impossible to determine just who said what. Dottie's contemporaries were particularly vulnerable: as another celebrated wit, the playwright and director George S. Kaufman, dolefully predicted, "Everything I've ever said will be credited to Dorothy Parker." But Woollcott's profile did create an abiding interest in cataloguing Parkerisms when he related the following anecdotes, among many others:

Dottie was recuperating in a hospital—aka "Bedpan Alley"—when thy was already as widely known for her tongue as for her pen, which she was, in later years Woollcott's essay would come to be viewed as an essential source for the thriving commerce in Parker Wit that ultimately overwhelmed any other public reputation that she earned.

Dorothy was only forty years old when the profile appeared. She already had published three collections of popular and well-received poetry. She was a prizewinning short-story writer, an influential literary and drama critic, and just then was negotiating a lucrative contract to write screenplays in Hollywood. But after "Our Mrs. Parker" she was a commodity of distinct proportions: the tiny woman with the big mouth who knew the gamut from A to B and wrote irreverent reviews that sounded as if she was still at the Algonquin Round Table; the one who also wrote a few poems, short stories, and film scripts whose titles were not quite so memorable as one might presume; the one who survived those abortions and suicide attempts and wretched affairs along the way and whose life often made her want to fwow up.

So much so that the artist was evolving into stock literary and theatrical cliché. In 1932, two years before the Woollcott profile, Dorothy was the model for "Lily Malone" in Philip Barry's play *Hotel Universe*. In Barry's description, Lily was "able to impart to her small, impudent face a certain prettiness." Also in 1932, Dorothy was "Mary Hilliard" in George Oppenheimer's *Here Today,* which was directed by George S. Kaufman, a former

---

Woollcott came to visit. Soon after he arrived she rang a bell. He asked if she was calling for drinks. "No, it is supposed to fetch the night nurse, so I ring it whenever I want an hour of uninterrupted privacy."

When she heard that an acquaintance had hurt herself in London, Dottie assumed the poor woman must have injured herself sliding down a barrister. And if all the girls who attended the Yale prom were laid end to end, Dottie insisted she would not be at all surprised.

Woollcott recalled that the unpopular wife of a "successful playwright" (Mary Sherwood) was forever discussing her pregnancy. When the baby was born, Dottie sent her a wire—collect: GOOD LUCK, MARY. WE ALL KNEW YOU HAD IT IN YOU.

Algonquin Round Table colleague of hers like Woollcott, but with whom Dorothy tended to share a cordial mutual antipathy.

In 1934, the year the Woollcott piece appeared, "Dorothy" starred as the dowdy "Julia Glenn" in the Kaufman–Moss Hart comedy *Merrily We Roll Along*. Julia was "a woman close to forty. She is not unpretty, but on her face are the marks of years and years of quiet and steady drinking—eight, ten hours a day." Also in 1934, she was the nightclub singer "Daisy Lester" in Charles Brackett's Algonquin roman à clef novel *Entirely Surrounded*, "a tiny, dark figure in a blue dress with peasant embroidery on the sleeves" who observed "what a dandy device life is for making people suffer . . . with other patents pending, I understand." And in 1944, she resurfaced as "Paula Wharton" in *Over 21,* a play written by the actress Ruth Gordon and again directed by Kaufman.[2] The die was cast. Dorothy Parker was famous for being Dorothy Parker, and in the popular consciousness that was what she would always be.

Dorothy Rothschild[3] was born, prematurely, on August 22, 1893, in West End, New Jersey.[4] Her mother, Eliza née Marston, descended from English Protestants; her father, Jacob Henry Rothschild, who preferred to be known by his middle name, was born in Selma, Alabama, of Prussian Jews. Henry was a partner in a prosperous cloak-making firm, and the family lived a comfortable life with servants in a good neighborhood on Manhattan's Upper West Side.

---

2. Dottie was not pleased by the sincerest form of flattery: "I suppose that now if I ever wrote a play about myself, I'd be sued for plagiarism." Another time, Dottie met a playwright she thought was appropriating some of her ideas. He said that his next work was a "play against all isms." Dottie: "Except plagiarism."

3. Dottie later confessed: "My God, *no,* dear! We'd never even heard of *those* Rothschilds!"

4. Dottie: "I was cheated out of the distinction of being a native New Yorker, because I had to go and get born while the family was spending the summer in New Jersey, but, honestly, we came back to New York right after Labor Day, so I nearly made the grade."

Eliza died a month before Dorothy's fifth birthday. Henry quickly married one Eleanor Lewis, but Dorothy disliked her—she claimed Eleanor was "crazy with religion"—and refused to call her "Mother." Years later Dorothy recalled an implausibly grim childhood with such standard elements as the distant father and the wicked stepmother, but more likely Dorothy was the "artistic" child who wrote verses and loved the assortment of dogs that the family adopted and then spoiled. She retained her love of undisciplined dogs and most other creatures[5] for the remainder of her life.[6] Eleanor died three years after she married Henry, when Dorothy was still only nine years old.

Dorothy was a small child: when she was twelve she was an inch less than five feet tall, and she never grew much taller. She was excessively thin and would remain underweight until

---

5. When Dottie was an adult she adopted two baby alligators without knowing quite what to do with them. So she left them in her bathtub until she could decide how to proceed. The next day she was out doing errands when her maid let herself in. Dottie returned to an uncleaned apartment and a note: "Dear Madam. I am leaving, as I cannot work in a house with alligators. I would have told you this before, but I never thought the subject would come up."

6. In later life Dottie had a dog called Woodrow Wilson. Woodrow suffered from what Aleck Woollcott delicately characterized as a "distressing malady." According to Dottie, the dog *said* he got it from a lamppost. She later adopted an amiable dachshund called Robinson. Robinson was attacked in the street by a much larger dog whose owner claimed that Robinson had started it. Dottie did not buy it: "I have no doubt that he was also carrying a revolver."

Once, Dottie brought her dog to a party where it vomited on the rug. Dottie: "It's the company." According to the late English raconteur Ned Sherrin, the great actress Mrs. Patrick Campbell exited a taxi with her dog in hand and a mess in the backseat. When the cabbie scolded her pet, Mrs. Pat claimed: "He didn't do it. I did." A variation of the story has Dottie delivering a similar response to the manager of the Beverly Hills Hotel after her dog messed the lobby.

Dottie's record with other animals was less commendable, though she once had a parakeet she called Onan. Why? See Genesis 38:9. But on another occasion a friend asked her how he could get rid of his cat. Dottie: "Have you tried curiosity?"

she was in her twenties, a quality she would recall nostalgically, and ruefully, in later years. She had a heart murmur. And she was an outsider both by temperament and circumstance. Although the Rothschilds identified as Jews, Henry first enrolled Dorothy in a Catholic elementary school, where she clashed with the nuns,[7] and then in a "restricted"—no Jews allowed—Protestant high school (Henry had lied about their background on the application). Dorothy left the high school six months later, when she was fourteen, and did not return. In the course of her formal education Dorothy had learned some Latin and French, and developed a keen appreciation for literature and poetry, but in later life she avoided admitting that she had never graduated high school.[8]

After leaving school Dorothy lived with her father for six increasingly grim years. Henry suffered financial reverses, grew ill, and finally died in 1913, when he was sixty-two and Dorothy was twenty. Though he bequeathed only a small estate to his four children (Dorothy was the youngest), he did leave something: Dorothy later claimed that she had been left penniless.

In 1914, she found work as a dance instructor to support herself while she nursed literary ambitions. She experimented with light verse and in 1915 sold a piece to Frank Crowninshield, who a year before had been appointed editor of the new *Vanity Fair* magazine by the publisher Condé Nast. In nine repetitive stanzas, "Any Porch" casually dissected the meandering conversations of upper-middle-class women of a certain age. Dorothy was paid twelve dollars for the piece and received her first known credit when *Vanity Fair* published it in the September 1915 issue. Moreover, Crowninshield evidently liked this

7. She later argued: "Well, how do you *expect* them to treat a kid who saw fit to refer to the Immaculate Conception as 'Spontaneous Combustion'? Boy, did I think I was smart! Still do."

8. Dottie: "The only thing I ever learned [in school] that ever did me any good in after life was that if you spit on a pencil eraser, it will erase ink."

unformed but promising young talent and, at Dorothy's urgent request, arranged for her a ten-dollar-a-week job writing captions at *Vanity Fair*'s sister publication *Vogue*.[9]

But working for *Vogue* in 1914, and for nearly forty years thereafter, meant working under Edna Woolman Chase, whose rigorous standard of decorum included white gloves and prohibited open-toed shoes. When an editor who had attempted suicide returned to work, Mrs. Chase called her in and explained to her the facts of death: "We at *Vogue* don't throw ourselves under subway trains, my dear. If we must, we take sleeping pills."

Dorothy was a seditious force who did not fit in with the *Vogue* staff.[10] Mrs. Chase did try to take advantage of Dorothy's talents,[11] and published a poem titled "The Lady in Back" in the November 1916 issue. And for her part Dorothy did volunteer for several weird experiments, including a risky new process called a permanent wave. But ultimately both Mrs. Chase and Dorothy concluded that Dorothy belonged somewhere else. In the fall of 1917, she moved down the hall to Crowninshield's *Vanity Fair*.

She had been submitting poems and verses to *Vanity Fair* for

---

9. More than forty years later, Dottie recalled the exhilaration of landing that first literary job at *Vogue*: "Well, I thought I was Edith Sitwell."

10. Dottie was astounded, but hardly speechless, the first time she saw the ornate *Vogue* offices: "Well, it looks just like the entrance to a house of ill-fame."

She wrote this caption for an underwear layout: "From these foundations of the autumn wardrobe, one may learn that brevity is the soul of lingerie, as the Petticoat said to the Chemise." That line actually appeared in the magazine, but the proofreaders caught and scrapped her caption for a photograph of a model wearing an expensive nightgown that suggested commercial, as well as romantic, considerations: "There was a little girl who had a little curl, right in the middle of her forehead. When she was good she was very, very good, and when she was bad she wore this divine nightdress of rose-colored mousseline de soie, trimmed with frothy Valenciennes lace."

11. When Mrs. Chase assigned her feature stories, Dottie often tried to embarrass her subjects, such as in "Interior Desecration," where she ridiculed the stereotype of a flamboyantly hysterical homosexual decorator.

years. None were particularly good: the next three that Crown-inshield published, "The Bridge Fiend," "A Musical Comedy Thought," and "The Gunman and the Débutante," had clever moments but still displayed more potential than competence. And one of them could have destroyed her career.

"A Musical Comedy Thought" appeared in the June 1916 issue of *Vanity Fair*. It described, with tongue firmly in cheek, a popular female impersonator who performed on the vaude-ville circuit. But then Franklin P. Adams interceded. Adams, the famous "F.P.A." of the *New York Tribune*, was New York's preeminent columnist. He also dabbled in poetry and published several highly regarded collections of light verse, which included "Baseball's Sad Lexicon," more familiarly known as "Tinker to Evers to Chance." Nearly every day that his "Conning Tower" column appeared he published submissions from readers who wanted to display their talents publicly, and the gold watch he awarded annually for the year's best poem was perhaps New York's most valued literary prize. And it was the mighty Frank Adams who, on May 23, 1916, took notice of young Dorothy Rothschild when he started his column with Dorothy's verse:

My heart is fairly melting at the thought of Julian Eltinge;
        His vice versa, Vesta Tilley, too.
Our language is so dexterous, let us call them ambi-sexterous,—
        Why hasn't this occurred before to you?

Adams followed it with his own devastating response:

In answer to your plotty little poem, Mistress Dotty,
It often has occurred to me, but then,
I thought it was absurd to steal a notion that occurred to
Percy Hammond in the spring of Nineteen Ten.

Close enough. Hammond was the *Chicago Tribune* drama critic when he praised "the ambisextrous Eltinge" in a review that appeared in December 1910. But Adams's indictment was harsh and overstated, and Dorothy was not "a plagiarist, at least implicitly," as was asserted in the introduction to the first edition of this collection. Attribution should be supplied where established custom and practice regard it reasonable to do so, but that clearly does not apply here. Dorothy used a fad word someone else coined. And we don't even know whether she read Hammond's review. She likely did not.

Which would have been scant consolation for her. What happened next? We don't know. There appears to be no record of the exchange outside the old "Conning Tower" clippings, and although there is no evidence that either Dorothy or Adams ever mentioned the incident again, it must have been a severe blow to her. She was only twenty-two, with a tenuous hold on an entry-level literary job, and was trying desperately to make a name for herself in that world. Instead, her first substantial public recognition was being accused of appropriating someone else's wit. Irony upon irony.

Dorothy had at least two similar but vastly less serious brushes with Adams in later years. In 1914, Adams had hailed Dulcinea, a popular recurring character in "The Conning Tower," with "Dulcy far niente," a pun on the Italian "dolce far niente," loosely translated as "pleasant idleness." Seven years later, in November 1921, Dorothy borrowed it for "Lynn Fontanne," a verse saluting the star of the hit George S. Kaufman–Marc Connelly comedy *Dulcy,* which was based on the same character. Although Adams surely recalled his earlier remark—he had a fabulous memory—he did not comment publicly on her appropriation. But he did preen while writing "To Dorothy Parker" in "The Conning Tower," which by then appeared in the New York *World,* on December 18, 1922:

You borrowed, about March Seventeen
"The Life and Death of Harriet Frean."

Adams probably was comparing the dreary title character in May Sinclair's *The Life and Death of Harriett Frean,* which had been published earlier that year, to the stock literary figure described in Dorothy's verse "The Drab Heroine," which had appeared in *Life* magazine earlier in 1922. But that was all far in the future when, in mid-1916, Dorothy must have felt severely chastened and was fretfully considering her next step.

She had probably been experimenting with free verse for some time before she surrendered to her caustic instincts and tried to write a screed. The result was "Women: A Hate Song," a broad and extended diatribe cataloguing the alleged faults of her own sex. Dorothy submitted it to Crowninshield under the name "Henriette Rousseau";[12] he published it in the August 1916 issue, and it evidently drew enough attention for Crowninshield to ask her for more like it. And over the next eight years Dorothy produced eighteen more so-called hate verses, all but one of them appearing either in *Vanity Fair* or *Life* magazine, skewering, among other targets, husbands and wives, actors and actresses, books, theater, and film. The series spawned several imitators.

That summer, Dorothy fell in love with Edward Pond Parker II, a tall, fair stockbroker from an old Connecticut Congregationalist family. She may have conducted casual affairs with similar men before—she always liked athletes with northwest European[13] features—but, she admitted forty years later, Eddie was "beautiful." He also was "not very smart. He was supposed to be in Wall Street, but that didn't mean anything."

When the United States entered the First World War in April 1917, Eddie enlisted in the army and proposed marriage. As Eddie's family disapproved of the match, and Dorothy already had distanced herself from her own family, neither side attended the June ceremony. Soon Eddie was called to active

12. Years later she signed some pieces "Helen Wells," probably a play on "Hell on Wheels."

13. Also years later, she ruefully described her "type": "I require only three things of a man. He must be handsome, ruthless, and stupid."

duty and learned to drive an ambulance.[14] While Eddie served in France, Dorothy kept the home fires burning by writing hate verses about bohemians and slackers who were not pulling their weight in the war effort.

Dorothy found a home at *Vanity Fair*. Crowninshield hoped to bring about a revival of Good Taste—it was said that his "mind was cultivated rather than profound"—and his purportedly frothy magazine was one of the most aesthetically beautiful yet adventurous publications of that or any era, on the very cusp of the avant-garde. During his first fifteen years there (during the sixteenth year he helped establish the Museum of Modern Art), *Vanity Fair* introduced a blinding array of new talent to the mass American public: "his" writers included Dorothy, Robert Benchley, P. G. Wodehouse, Edna St. Vincent Millay, e. e. cummings, and Aldous Huxley. Crowninshield took particular pride in *Vanity Fair*'s visual "look," which often startled traditional sensibilities. Though he brought artists such as Rockwell Kent, Pablo Picasso, and Miguel Covarrubias to public attention, Crowninshield ruefully observed in 1928 that "the new artists whom we have periodically presented have aroused the greater part of the criticism that *Vanity Fair* has had to combat from time to time." Crowninshield also employed photographers such as Baron (Adolf) de Meyer and Edward Steichen "when their work was branded as wild and absurd."

Dorothy worked as a general editorial assistant for several months, but when Wodehouse took a leave of absence Crowninshield appointed her drama critic. She may not have been the first female drama critic, but she was the only one in New York at that time. She started her column in the April 1918 issue and, as with the hate verses, she found she preferred inflicting abuse to tendering praise.[15] She was amusing, she was witty, she was

14. Dottie: "We were married for about five minutes, then he went off to war."

15. Though most of her reviews were innocuous, there were notable exceptions. In her very first column, in April 1918, she suggested attending

wicked, and she was noticed. People started talking about that terrible Mrs. Parker.

In November the war ended, but Eddie remained in Europe with the occupation forces. Dorothy continued reviewing plays and submissions while Crowninshield searched for a managing editor. What he found was a seemingly prim and reserved twenty-nine-year-old teetotaler who had written some of the funniest pieces Crowninshield had ever read. On May 19, 1919, Dorothy arrived at work to meet Robert Benchley: he introduced himself to "Mrs. Parker," she greeted "Mr. Benchley," and they set to work, more or less.

A few days later Crowninshield introduced their new "drama editor," with unspecified duties: a young (twenty-three) and towering (six feet seven inches tall) veteran of the Canadian Black Watch regiment called Robert Sherwood. If Benchley was relatively reticent, Sherwood was silent—so quiet, in fact, that he scared his new coworkers.[16] It turned out that Sherwood was very shy, and as he relaxed, the three quickly forged close friendships.

Perhaps they got on *too* well: eight months later, none of them still worked at *Vanity Fair*. "I must say we behaved extremely badly," Dorothy admitted later. She and Benchley subscribed to undertakers' magazines and posted diagrams over her desk. They set their own hours, which caused Nast to institute "tardy slips," which caused Benchley to submit one explaining that he had run eleven minutes late while saving the city from rampag-

---

Girl o' Mine "if you want a couple of hours' undisturbed rest. If you don't knit, bring a book." As to *The Love Mill,* "I know who wrote those lyrics and I know the names of the people in the cast, but I'm not going to tell on them." *Sinbad,* she concluded, was "produced in accordance with the fine old Shubert precept that nothing succeeds like undress," which was, at least, an improvement over the production whose chorus line appeared to be composed of "kind, motherly-looking women."

16. Dottie warned Benchley that Sherwood was a "Conversation Stopper." In a light piece she had published in *Vanity Fair* a few months earlier she warned that talking with a Conversation Stopper was like "riding on the Long Island Railroad—it gets you nowhere in particular."

ing elephants. When both Crowninshield and Nast were traveling, Benchley allowed Sherwood to print outlandish fashion predictions. When they were ordered not to discuss their salaries, they wrote the relevant numbers on posterboard and wore them around their necks.

In December, Sherwood was fired. In January, Crowninshield dismissed Dorothy on the stated grounds that Wodehouse was returning and she no longer was needed. Dorothy suspected she really had been fired for offending prominent producers with her harsh reviews, in particular her relatively mild criticism of Billie Burke's (Mrs. Florenz Ziegfeld) performance in *Caesar's Wife*. (Nineteen years later Ms. Burke played Glinda, the Good Witch of the North, in *The Wizard of Oz*.) Prominent producers were also prominent advertisers. "*Vanity Fair* was a magazine of no opinion, and *I* had opinions," Dorothy said much later.[17] Benchley immediately resigned in protest, though he was barely solvent and had to support a wife and two young children. Dorothy called it "the greatest act of friendship I'd known." For all their highly publicized bitterness, however, all three were submitting material to *Vanity Fair* a few years later,[18] and Dorothy published nine poems there in 1926.

In the January 12, 1920, entry in his "Diary of Our Own Samuel Pepys," a weekly feature of "The Conning Tower," Frank Adams reported to New York in faux-Restoration language that "R. Benchley tells me he hath resigned his position with 'Vanity Fair' because they hath discharged Mistress Doro-

---

17. After leaving *Vanity Fair,* Dottie ran across Nast in the Algonquin lobby. Nast was a notorious libertine, and he asked her to join him on an ocean cruise. She politely declined; then, as soon as he left, turned to the critic Edmund Wilson: "Oh, God, make that ship sink!"

18. For example, both Dottie and Sherwood participated when *Vanity Fair* asked literary celebrities to compose their own epitaphs for the October 1924 issue. Her entry: "Here Lies the Body of Dorothy Parker. Thank God!" At other times she suggested different closing thoughts, including, "Excuse my dust," "This is on me," and "If you can read this you've come too close."

thy Parker; which I am sorry for." Adams no longer considered Dorothy the appropriating upstart he had dismissed less than four years before. She was a colleague, even a friend, someone with whom he had something very useful in common: Dorothy, along with Benchley, and Sherwood, and Adams himself, was a member of the celebrated Round Table of the Algonquin Hotel in midtown Manhattan.

The Round Table had started six months earlier, in June 1919, when thirty-five so-called friends attended a luncheon celebrating Alexander Woollcott's return from the First World War, where he had served in Paris on the staff of the military newspaper, *Stars and Stripes*. Woollcott was a *New York Times* drama critic before volunteering for the army, and while he may already have known Adams before going overseas, they had developed a friendship during the several months they spent together on the army paper.

Also present at the luncheon was another former *Stars and Stripes* staffer, Harold Ross of Aspen, Colorado. Though Woollcott took inordinate pleasure in baiting the tumultuous Ross, he also had introduced him to Jane Grant, whom Ross would eventually marry. Heywood Broun, the popular columnist, was also there. Broun had worked with Adams at the *New York Tribune* and had also traveled to France during the war, though Broun went there as a civilian correspondent. He would continue to work with Adams for most of the next decade at the *Tribune* and then at Herbert Bayard Swope's *World*. A few years after the luncheon, Jane Grant and Broun's wife, Ruth Hale, would form the Lucy Stone League, a feminist organization committed to establishing the right of women to retain their maiden names after marriage.[19]

The journalists George S. Kaufman (*New York Times*) and Marc Connelly (*New York Morning Telegraph*) had both migrated

19. Dottie once sent a wire: TO RUTH BROUN FROM DOROTHY ROTHSCHILD.

to New York from western Pennsylvania, and would soon collaborate on light theatrical comedies. Their first big hit would be the aforementioned *Dulcy*. They did not attend the first luncheon, but were soon regular members of the Table. The press agents John Peter Toohey and Murdock Pemberton attended the homecoming, and would both continue to appear for several years. The Table also would eventually welcome the novelist Edna Ferber and the comic writer Donald Ogden Stewart. The popular cover artist Neysa McMein, a statuesque advocate of open marriage,[20] was a frequent and valued visitor; so were Margaret (Peggy) Leech, who later married the *World*'s owner—a Pulitzer—and then won two Pulitzer Prizes for history, and Margalo Gillmore, a lively young actress for whom Marc Connelly nurtured a passion that she could not, or at least did not, reciprocate. (Miss Gillmore was the Table's last survivor; she died in 1986, aged eighty-nine.) Two of the most famous "Algonks," Swope and Ring Lardner, actually were not: both took care to avoid the lunches, although they often attended the Saturday night poker auxiliary, the Thanatopsis Literary and Inside Straight Club.

Most of those who comprised the nucleus of the Table were similarly situated: they were relatively young, between twenty-five and thirty-five years old; they were from somewhere else (except Broun and, for all practical purposes, Dorothy) but were desperately anxious to be taken for Manhattan sophisticates; they worked in what would much later be called the communications and entertainment industries; they were ambitious; and they were willing to engage in mutual back-scratching for personal benefit. Their critics called it logrolling.

The primary means at their disposal was wit: wit accumulated for the next lunch; wit for the next morning's newspapers or the

---

20. Dottie helped a nervous married friend prepare for his first tryst with Neysa, even taking him to the pharmacy to buy condoms. Then he felt compelled to tell her that it was his first infidelity. Dottie: "Oh, don't worry, I'm sure it won't be the last."

next day's rehearsals; wit that could get plays produced, or jobs offered, or newspapers sold. Dorothy was a particularly visible member, though thirty years later she unconvincingly claimed that she "wasn't there very often—it cost too much."[21] But, like so much of her recollection of her past life, it is opportunely inaccurate. She ate lunch there regularly and tended to socialize with other Algonks the remainder of the time. When Noël Coward encountered the same crowd three times in three different places on the same day, he asked, "Don't they ever see anyone bloody else?"

Dorothy preferred to lurk in the background. She liked to think of herself as a lady, too mannered to shout, or even to raise her voice, like so many of the others. She felt no compulsion to flaunt her wit. And when she did have something she wanted to say—usually some understated ferocity—she characteristically delivered it in a low, hesitant, almost diffident murmur,[22] with a deadpan expression that enormously heightened the effect of the words. But for all the protestations that she only intended to deflate the pompous or to humble the arrogant, there was such a gratuitous and even gleeful streak of calculated cruelty to so many of her attacks on less articulate victims that there is no reason to conclude that her primary motive was anything more than to humiliate people who had done her no harm, just because she was able and was expected to do so.

Eddie returned to New York in August 1919. He had been a heavy drinker before he sailed with his unit (his pallor caused his army buddies to nickname him "Spook"), but during the war his alcoholism had spiraled out of control. It was clear very soon after he came home that Dorothy had lost interest[23] in him. She

---

21. In a 1959 television interview, during the course of her campaign to revise her role at the Round Table, Dottie quipped that "most of them are dead now, but they weren't too alive then."

22. She once said that "a girl's best friend is her mutter."

23. Dottie claimed to possess a low threshold for bores, but she took great care to find them wherever she went because they were such good material. Of one she said: "He's the type of man who is sure to keep the

claimed that he had returned from France with a morphine addiction, which may have been true—but likely not—and she publicly ridiculed him by introducing him as "my little husband" and, when he was absent, by portraying him as the hapless victim of a series of horrible misadventures that had never occurred.[24] Marc Connelly recalled that Eddie was "a quiet, pleasant young man who was out of his element. He couldn't keep up with Dottie."

She appeared to describe the state of her marriage in her verse. First she seemed willing to try to make it work (though she likely had already engaged in an adulterous affair); "Fragment" appeared in the *Life* issue dated January 12, 1922:

> *It is the quest that thrills, and not the gain,*
> *The mad pursuit, and not the cornering:*
> *Love caught is but a drop of April rain,*
> *But bloom upon the moth's translucent wing.*
> *Why should you dare to hope that you and I*
> *Could make love's fitful flash a lasting flame?*
> *Still, if you think it's only fair to try—*
> *Well, I am game.*

But things quickly changed. In March 1922 she sold "Day-Dreams" to *Life*—and it concluded:

> *If you and I were one, my dear,*
> *A model life we'd lead.*

conversation ho-humming." Another asked if she'd had her ears pieced: "No, but I have often had them bored."

24. Dottie's first biographer John Keats catalogued a few: he dropped through a manhole while walking down the street reading the *Wall Street Journal*. He broke his arm sharpening a pencil. Once they arrived at a funeral a half-hour early and found themselves alone in a room with the body. As Keats put it: "Eddie began to fool around with a knob beneath the casket, and machinery began to hum, the casket began to move, a door opened—and casket and corpse went neatly and quietly into the hot little hell of the crematory." They fled. According to Dottie, that is.

We'd travel on, from year to year,
At no increase of speed.
Ah, clear to me the vision of
The things that we should do!
And so I think it best, my love,
To string along as two.

They separated soon after, and with the exception of a failed reconciliation two years later, they lived separate lives before they finally divorced in 1928.[25] Eddie remarried but died of an accidental overdose of sleeping powders in 1933, aged only thirty-nine.

After leaving *Vanity Fair,* Dorothy and Benchley rented a tiny[26] triangular office near Times Square in the Metropolitan Opera House studios for thirty dollars a month, where they joked about the future[27] while trying to figure out just what to do with it. Dorothy wrote theater reviews for the literary *Ainslee's Magazine* and worked freelance for the *Saturday Evening Post* and *Ladies Home Journal.* Benchley wrote advertising copy and occasional book reviews for the *World.* In April 1920, Benchley followed Sherwood to *Life,* a sophisticated humor magazine, where he was appointed drama critic. Dorothy started submitting her rhymes there in September, and over the next three years she sold nearly one hundred verses to *Life* and the *Saturday Evening Post.* It was more commerce than art,[28] as she frankly

---

25. Dottie recalled that they got the divorce "in Connecticut, where you can get it for roller skating." The night the divorce came through, Dottie and her new boyfriend, John Garrett II, went to Jack and Charlie's Puncheon Club and met some friends. When Garrett got up and said he was going to the bathroom, Dottie muttered: "He really needs to telephone, but he's too embarrassed to say so."

26. Dottie: "An inch smaller and it would have been adultery. We had *Parkbench* for a cable address, but no one ever sent us one."

27. They considered having their door lettered: UTICA DROP FORGE AND TOOL CO., ROBERT BENCHLEY, PRESIDENT—DOROTHY PARKER, PRESIDENT.

28. She put it quite succinctly in February 1928, in the guise of the *New*

declared in "The Far-Sighted Muse," which appeared in *Life* in March 1922 (and that displayed the parenthesized aside that had been employed by the nineteenth-century English poet Thomas Hood, one of her favorites):

> *Smile, and the World will smile back at you;*
> > *Aim with a grin, and you cannot miss;*
> *Laugh off your woes, and you won't feel blue.*
> > *(Poetry pays when it's done like this.)*

She also wrote a few prose pieces for *Life* and other magazines, but not as many as she could have written, for they took far more time and effort than the verses and she lacked the discipline to do so. The quality of her poetry improved vastly with practice, and she became more proficient with the mechanics of the surprise or incongruous ending. It was soon her most characteristic touch. Readers learned to wait until the very last line of a stanza, or even of an entire piece, because it often contradicted all that had preceded it. This device, mastered by Horace in the classical era, recently had become popular again, possibly through the critical success that attended the English writer H. H. Munro ("Saki"), who often employed it in the polished short stories that he wrote during the first decade of the century. Munro had been killed during the last stages of the battle of the Somme in 1916, and his work was just becoming familiar to cosmopolitan American readers in the mid-twenties.

But no matter how well she was received, Dorothy stubbornly refused to accept praise for her work. In 1956 she declared that she only wrote "verses. I cannot say poems. Like everybody was then, I was following in the exquisite footsteps of Miss Millay,

Yorker's "Constant Reader" looking for work: "Salary is no object; I want only enough to keep body and soul apart."

Five years earlier, in the June 1923 *Ainslee's,* she had calculated when she would be a millionaire: "I figure, by the way things are running now, I ought to have it piled up somewhere around the late spring of 2651."

unhappily in my own horrible sneakers. Let's face it, honey, my verse is horribly dated—as anything once fashionable is dreadful now." But what was once "horribly dated" could again become fashionable, as happened after her death.

As her interest in Eddie waned, she spent more and more time with the other Algonks. Her close but probably platonic relationship with Benchley generated rumors that never quite disappeared, and Gertrude Benchley feared and hated her.[29] Dorothy liked Neysa McMein, whose studio was across the hall from the Parkers' apartment. Neysa's was the usual Algonk late-afternoon haunt, and likely was New York's leading salon of the time: Dorothy could expect to find Bernard Baruch or Herbert Bayard Swope conversing there with Paul Robeson or Noël Coward while George Gershwin or Irving Berlin provided background music while Anaïs Nin posed for Neysa. Dorothy was a frequent visitor even after she moved to the Algonquin in October 1925.[30]

Frequent references in "The Conning Tower" and talk around town caused Dorothy to develop a formidable reputation for repartee at the Algonquin, at Neysa's, at Swope's palatial Man-

29. Many women thought that Dottie was particularly hard on her own sex. Much has been written about her purportedly celebrated feud with the editor and writer Clare Boothe Brokaw, later Luce. Dottie was even said to have mocked her name—"'Clare—Boothe—Luce'—sounds like the motto of a girl's school"—but Dottie almost certainly did not say the other things she was supposed to have said about her. So there is no reason to relate these two famous stories: First, that when they converged at a doorway, Clare smiled and stepped aside: "Age before beauty," and Dottie strolled through the door: "And pearls before swine." And second, at a dinner party, the actress Ilka Chase (the daughter of the *Vogue* editor Edna Woolman Chase) defended Clare by asserting that not only was Clare loyal to her friends, but "she's very kind to her inferiors." Dottie: "And where does she find them?"

30. She seldom paid her rent on time. According to the writer Joe Bryan, a friend once asked her: "Did you hang up your stocking on Christmas Eve?" Dottie: "No, I hung up my hotel."

One time the Algonquin's owner and manager, Frank Case, called her when he heard reports that she was breaking a house rule: "Do you have a gentleman in your room?" Dottie: "Just a minute. I'll ask him."

hattan apartment and even more opulent Great Neck estate (reputedly the model for Fitzgerald's Gatsby's),[31] at other country houses,[32] at dinners and parties,[33] playing games,[34] and just walking down the street.[35] But she was also secretly despised and feared by many people in her circle for what Edmund Wilson called her "treachery": she was notorious for conversing cordially

---

31. At one of Swope's Halloween parties, when Dottie asked why several people were standing around a washtub, she was told that "they're ducking for apples." Dottie: "There, but for a typographical error, is the story of my life." At another Swope party Dottie was talking with Maryland governor Albert Ritchie when someone at the table belched. There was a moment of strained silence, then . . . Dottie: "I'll get the Governor to pardon you."

32. Dottie found herself traveling to Long Island more than she professed to enjoy, as she complained in a 1927 *Life* piece: "No matter where I go, I always have to change at Jamaica." (Jamaica was, and still is, the central train terminal in Queens.)

In 1925 the actress Fay Bainter boasted that she had been married to her husband for seven years. Dottie: "Don't worry, he'll come back in style again."

When Aleck Woollcott and Dottie spent a weekend at Ruth Hale's dilapidated country house in Connecticut, they found an old battered toothbrush hanging from a nail over the basin, presumably supplied for communal use. Woollcott: "In God's name, what do you suppose [Ruth] does with that?" Dottie studied the thing for a moment: "I think she rides on it on Halloween."

33. The writer Charles MacArthur was wearing a white cotton suit, smoking a thin cigar, and holding a frosted glass when Dottie approached him at a summer party: "As the American consul here, sir—" She once dismissed a wealthy vulgarian as "a rhinestone in the rough."

34. Dottie excelled at the popular Algonquin game where the players challenged each other to use a long word in a punning sentence. She was challenged with "horticulture." Dottie: "You can lead a horticulture, but you can't make her think." She was challenged with "paroxysm." Dottie: "Paroxysm agnificent city." And in a 1927 book review: "I think I'm going to be able to use 'opium' in a sentence. I opium mother is feeling better. No, I guess I'm not, either."

Her musical variant: "Do you know the celery song: 'Celery gather at the river?' Or the Irish song, 'Irish I was in Dixie?' How about the French one? '*Je suis* have no bananas?' Or the Spanish national anthem? 'Jose, can you see?'" And her question during a spirited game of Twenty Questions: "Would he be the kind of man who would put the wings back on flies?"

35. She hailed a taxi but the cabbie said: "I'm engaged." Dottie: "Then be happy."

with someone one moment and then, as soon as his back was turned, attacking him—or more likely her—the next.[36]

Dorothy's alcohol consumption steadily increased, and when she went out to drink she usually was accompanied by Benchley or Heywood Broun. Before 1921 Benchley was a teetotaler who warned Dorothy that drink would "coarsen" her, but he eventually took up the habit himself and eventually deteriorated into a compulsive alcoholic, adulterer, and spendthrift. They usually drank at speakeasies such as Tony Soma's[37] (Tony was the maternal grandfather of the actress Anjelica Huston) or Jack and Charlie's Puncheon Club, later the restaurant 21. Dorothy eventually settled upon "her" drink—Johnny Walker Scotch whiskey neat—spacing her sips so that she seldom was completely drunk, but seldom perfectly sober, either.[38] She would drink too much in little sips the rest of her life.

Charles MacArthur moved to New York in 1921. He was two years younger than Dorothy, a charmer and a brawler, a star reporter from the hard-boiled Chicago school that he and Ben Hecht brought to life a few years later in the 1928 Broadway hit *The Front Page*. Soon Aleck Woollcott introduced Charlie to Dorothy—and sparks flew. Everyone warned Dorothy that Charlie was only looking for a good time. Neysa McMein had given him a rubber

---

36. Just after a woman left the room, Dottie started to discuss her. A friend of the victim protested that the woman would not hurt a fly. Dottie: "Not if it was buttoned up."

On another occasion Dottie was particularly affable as she saw off a departing guest. Then: "That woman speaks eighteen languages, and can't say 'No' in any of them."

37. Dorothy and Benchley were accosted there one night by a customer who showed them a watch that he claimed was indestructible. They pounded the watch on the table, stamped on it, and then tested it some more. Finally the watch's owner grabbed it and put it to his ear: "It's stopped." They answered in unison: "Maybe you wound it too tight."

38. During the twenties, possibly at Tony Soma's, the bartender asked: "What are you having?" Dottie: "Not much fun." Another time her good friend John V. A. Weaver, the poet, presumed to tell her that she was looking well. Dottie: "Where the hell are you looking?"

stamp etched with "I LOVE YOU" to streamline his personal correspondence. Dorothy knew he was married. Yet she fell desperately in love with Charlie nonetheless. In doing so she established a cheerless pattern that she repeated with several men over the next decade: she beseeched, he parried; she whined, he withdrew; she accused, he cheated; she sobbed, he left.

Without naming names, Dorothy memorialized the MacArthur liaison in a potent poem she called "Pollyanna Gets the Air." (A "Pollyanna" "is unduly optimistic or achieves happiness through self-delusion," per the *Oxford English Dictionary*; it derives from the sunny title character of Eleanor H. Porter's 1913 bestseller *Pollyanna*. "To get the air" was period slang for being jilted.) Dorothy sold "Pollyanna" to *Life* in January 1922—evidently Charlie had already dropped her by then—but it did not run until the June 22 issue. And it appeared anonymously, without any credit whatever. Did Dorothy ask that her name be removed? Or did Robert Sherwood, then a junior but influential *Life* editor, quietly delete Dorothy's byline to insulate her from gossip? Or . . . ? No doubt she *was* vulnerable: her affair with MacArthur was widely discussed within her circle and beyond, and from the first line she made clear that this was raw and personal stuff, indeed:

> *So many others had gone before—*
> > *Didn't I know that I'd not be last?*
> *So many names on his heart he wore—*
> > *Didn't I know it would soon be past? . . .*
> *Give him my love.*

Dorothy's romantic disasters puzzled many observers. Most men found her quite attractive, even after her weight started to fluctuate. The fastidious Edmund Wilson was entranced by her sexual allure but later professed to have been repelled by her. She was small (various accounts put her height between four feet eleven inches and five feet four inches) yet voluptuous, with fine features that were dominated by huge dark eyes and, when she was so motivated, an often pleasant and even deferential demeanor. Yet she was probably describing herself as well as the flamboyant Isadora Duncan in a revealing 1928 *New Yorker* review: "She had a knack for selecting the unworthy—perhaps all great women have; one and all, they treated her with an extraordinary shabbiness." If MacArthur did not treat her shabbily, he was at the very least recklessly unconcerned about the pain that she was enduring.

Dorothy learned that she was pregnant and had an abortion,[39] but MacArthur already had moved on to newer and, he hoped, less fertile conquests. Finally, deeply depressed and drinking heavily, she appeared to attempt suicide by slashing her wrists with one of Eddie's old razors—but only after calling a local restaurant to deliver her dinner. The deliveryman found her and rushed her to the hospital in time to save her life.[40] Many of her friends thought she had done it to gain attention, and that is at least partly true. Over the next ten years she would appear to try to do away with herself at least three more times. First she swallowed an overdose of the sedative Veronal, but then she threw the drinking glass through a window, which drew timely attention. Then she swallowed a bottle of shoe polish, which was messy but not lethal. Then she tried sleeping powders, but did not consume a large enough dose to cause severe harm.[41]

After that first suicide attempt, Dorothy occasionally wore the

---

39. The rumor mill buzzed with the story. Dottie: "It serves me right for putting all my eggs in one bastard." Another rumor had MacArthur putting up thirty dollars toward the abortion, which, according to Dottie, was like Judas making a refund.

40. At the hospital Dottie decorated her bandaged wrists with pale blue ribbons and then with black velvet ribbons and large bows: "I suppose you might as well know. I slashed my wrists. Eddie doesn't even have a sharp razor."

41. After that last attempt, in 1932, she recuperated at a woman friend's country estate, where she was so buffeted by attention that she fired off a despairing telegram to a possible rescuer: FOR HEAVEN'S SAKE, RUSH ME A LOAF OF BREAD, ENCLOSING SAW AND FILE.

scent of tuberose, which traditionally was used by undertakers on corpses. Her poetry also assumed a less breezy and topical tone. In March 1923 she published a poem called "Triolet" (retitled "Triolet [1]" here):

> Give back the heart that I gave;
> > Keeping it never can mend it.
> See, I can smile, and be brave.
> Give back the heart that I gave,
> Hold it no more as your slave—
> > I've got a new place to send it.
> Give back the heart that I gave;
> > Keeping it never can mend it.

Over the ensuing decade a too-lengthy succession of men would share Dorothy's bed.[42] Marc Connelly described one of them as "dandruff." Many of the affairs, including those with Deems Taylor, F. Scott Fitzgerald,[43] and possibly even Ring Lardner (his family was "skeptical" of the rumor) and Frank Adams, were transitory arrangements. Other lovers, particularly the gentle and generous pornography collector Seward Collins and the more virile Johns— Garrett and McClain—would endure longer. Most would follow the MacArthur pattern, and none would last.[44] As it happened,

---

42. Reviewing a book of dating strategies in 1928, Dottie ruefully admitted that had she just played coquettish games, "maybe I could have been successful, instead of just successive."

43. Dottie met Fitzgerald through Edmund Wilson, who arranged a group lunch at the Algonquin. They were seated at a long and narrow table, one next to the other, with their backs to the wall. Dottie: "This looks like a road company of the Last Supper."

In 1940, by then a ruined man, Fitzgerald died in Hollywood, aged only forty-four. At the funeral, Dottie looked at him in his coffin and repeated the famous line from the funeral of the title character of Fitzgerald's most noteworthy book, The Great Gatsby: "The poor son-of-a-bitch."

44. McClain preferred wealthy women. At a cocktail party, Dottie shrugged after hearing him make a date with another woman. Dottie: "I have

both MacArthur and McClain, two of the three men who broke her heart, later moved in with her best friend, Robert Benchley.

A friend was later quoted as saying that Dorothy "was ignorant about money. All she knew was that she needed it." She often forgot to pay her taxes. She was a dreadful housekeeper and did not know how to cook. Someone said that she ate bacon raw because she did not know how to fry it. She spent whatever she earned, usually on scents, cigarettes, liquor, and clothes[45]—she loved hats—and was known to admit nearly everyone to the continuing drinks party at her apartment so long as they brought bottles with them.[46]

She always had aspired to be a recognized poet and a successful playwright. The increasing quality of the work she was publishing in *Life,* the *Saturday Evening Post,* and, by early 1923, Frank Adams's "Conning Tower" column in the *World,* lent increasing credibility to that first ambition. For the second, in early 1924 she convinced the successful playwright Elmer Rice to collaborate with her on a project she had started. She slept with him several times to seal the arrangement. She did not find the former Elmer Reizenstein attractive—he was Jewish, and looked it—but she managed to break off the affair without interfering with the play, which was called *Close Harmony*. They persuaded the prominent producer Arthur Hopkins to stage it, but it failed nonetheless.[47]

---

no squash courts. What can I do?" McClain left her for a rich Long Island hostess. Dottie: "He'll be back as soon as he has licked all the gilt off her ass." Her final verdict: "His body has gone to his head."

45. Dottie appeared to be shocked when she was told that an acquaintance was wearing a cape trimmed with monkey fur: "Really? I thought they were beards."

46. Dottie: "All I need is room enough to lay a hat and a few friends." One time a very drunk friend staggered in, emitting a succession of weird sounds as he struggled to speak. Dottie: "He thinks in French."

47. Dottie noticed that Hopkins was examining the actress Wanda Lyon's bouncing breasts during a dress rehearsal. Hopkins: "Dorothy, don't you think she ought to wear a brassiere in this scene?" Dottie: "God, no. You've got to have something in the show that moves." And when it became clear

Perhaps it wasn't the quality of the play that doomed it, but unfortunate timing: it opened on Broadway December 1, the same week as four big hits: Irving Berlin's newest *Music Box Revue,* Adele and Fred Astaire's *Lady, Be Good!* (with music from the Gershwins), Avery Hopwood's *The Harem,* and Sigmund Romberg's *The Student Prince of Heidelberg.* Despite excellent reviews, *Close Harmony* grossed less than ten thousand dollars before closing after four weeks and only twenty-four performances. Dorothy was crushed. Her verdict: "It was dull. You have my apologies."[48]

Meanwhile, Harold Ross somehow had persuaded the baking heir Raoul Fleischmann to subsidize his new cosmopolitan weekly magazine, which would be called the *New Yorker.* To help induce Fleischmann to invest, Ross convinced Dorothy and several other well-known Algonquin friends to join a "board of editors" of the magazine.[49] She published "Cassandra Drops Into

---

that the play was failing, she wired Robert Benchley: CLOSE HARMONY DID A COOL NINETY DOLLARS AT THE MATINEE. ASK THE BOYS IN THE BACK ROOM WHAT THEY WILL HAVE.

A few years later, in 1927, the hit flapper film *It* was released, which caused the Brooklyn-born star Clara Bow to be dubbed "The 'It' Girl." Bow was flummoxed when someone asked her what "It" was: "Well, I ain't real sure." But Dottie knew: "'It'? Hell, she had 'Those'!"

48. Dottie never lost her love for the theater and its characters. She particularly enjoyed Tallulah Bankhead's scandalous flamboyance, as when she inquired after Tallulah was particularly obstreperous at a party: "Has Whistler's Mother left yet?" Dottie visited the star's dressing room after an opening-night performance: "Tallulah, your show is slipping."

Dottie once sent a congratulatory first-night telegram to the actress Uta Hagen: A HAND ON YOUR OPENING AND MAY YOUR PARTS GROW BIGGER. But another time Dottie was goaded beyond endurance by an aging actress who had not worked in twenty years but still felt compelled to assure Dottie that "I just simply loathe the idea of leaving the theater, I'm so wedded to it." Dottie: "Why don't you sue, then, for non-support?"

49. The *New Yorker* survived its early desperate years only through ruthless economy. Decades later Dottie told Truman Capote: "Of course Harold Ross invented the *New Yorker*—who but a Colorado hillbilly could be so stingy?" During that first summer of 1925 Ross found Dottie in a speakeasy and asked why she was not producing copy instead. Dottie: "Someone was using the pencil."

Verse" in the magazine's second issue in February 1925, and over the remainder of the decade she sold to Ross more than fifty more poems and many prose pieces.

But in 1925, Dorothy was publishing most of her work without payment in Frank Adams's "Conning Tower" in the *World*.[50] On August 16, in the *Sunday World,* she published "Some Beautiful Letters," six verses that included her two most famous pieces: "News Item" ("Men seldom make passes / At girls who wear glasses"), whose creation she forever lamented as "a terrible thing" for a person with serious literary ambitions; and the jauntily autobiographical "Résumé" (" . . . Guns aren't lawful; / Nooses *all* give; / Gas smells awful; / You might as well live"), which was edited to its familiar form. Both were immediate sensations, but Dorothy's increasing fame also spawned some petty artistic jealousy.

Adams had many other frequent contributors, including one Elspeth MacDuffie O'Halloran (pen name "Elspeth"), whose work was similar, but inferior, to Dorothy's. Adams reported in his November 17, 1926, Diary entry that "unless somebody should be John Milton in a few days" he was going to give that year's coveted watch to Dorothy for "The Dark Girl's Rhyme."[51] Adams's announcement was evidently more than Elspeth could bear, because she soon submitted a challenge "To Dorothy Parker." After declaring her own literary burden in stanza one, and whin-

---

50. The humorist Frank Sullivan took the helm of "The Conning Tower" when Frank Adams left on a two-month honeymoon in May 1925. More than forty years later, just after Dottie died, Sullivan recalled that he "had a hell of a time filling that column. Dotty heard about it at Swope's or Tony Soma's or somewhere, or with her intuition sensed it from reading my flounderings, and by God one day two poems arrived from her! I still remember the note she sent with them: 'If you can't use these, give them to some poor family.'" She later sent Sullivan two more poems.

51. Also in the Diary entry for the same date, Adams related that "Dorothy Parker came to see me, and I overjoyed to see her, and she told me about her peregrinations abroad, and I asked her about Ernest Hemingway, and how old he was, and she said, 'Well, I don't know. You know, all writers are either twenty-nine or Thomas Hardy.'" Hardy was eighty-six at the time.

ing that Dorothy was columnist's pet in stanza two, Elspeth got to the point—Adams's watch prediction—in stanza three:

> *Of course, I'm glad it's Dorothy.*
> *I'm thrilling with delight.*
> *But how I'd like to meet that girl*
> *Alone some ebon night!*

It ran November 23. Dorothy was drinking very heavily and was deeply depressed at the time. She had recently made her second suicide attempt (Veronal) and was seeing a psychiatrist,[52] but she responded "To Elspeth" in "The Conning Tower" the next day:

> *Lady, I have read your verse on*
> *Me—the one wherein you write*
> *"How I'd like to meet that person*
> *All alone some ebon night!"*

> *Though your wish to wound were little,*
> *You have done your worst—you see,*
> *Some one, when my heart was brittle,*
> *Said those very words to me.*

> *Lady, take my humble greetings;*
> *Take my thanks; but let me say*
> *Were it not for midnight meetings,*
> *I'd be on my feet to-day.*

---

52. She soon stopped seeing the psychiatrist, Alvan Barach, because "I've never seen a cure." Her good friend Oscar Levant, the noted pianist and wit, also was treated by Barach. Once Levant asked Dottie if she took sleeping pills. Yes, she replied, "in a big bowl with sugar and cream."

Levant later shuttled in and out of psychiatric hospitals, including one that served dinner at 4:45 p.m. Dottie: "That makes for a nice long evening." Dottie on Levant: "He long ago said everything about everything—and what Oscar Levant has said, *stays* said."

A friend once said of her that "Dottie can only do her best work when her heart is breaking" and, at the time of the Elspeth scrap, Dorothy was preparing her first book of collected verse. Though she was convinced that her work was "not good enough" to be published in book form, Horace Liveright of the publishing house Boni & Liveright already had commissioned a similar project with another popular writer of light verse, Samuel Hoffenstein, and was confident that her collection would succeed. In early 1926 he broached the subject. Dorothy realized that the book could subsidize a long trip to Europe, so she agreed to supply a manuscript.

She felt that very little of her early work was good enough to appear in the book. While it tended to be less polished than her more recent product, in retrospect it is also clear that she deliberately chose to include those verses whose substance and style reflected what she hoped to project as her own, that is, the scarred and astringent modern woman, spare and unadorned, making her way through a new and starkly modern world, experienced in sex but cynical of love, defying all comers with a quip and a sneer— or a private sigh. Dorothy Parker usually felt most confident of her artistic abilities when she was writing about Dorothy Parker.

Dorothy ruthlessly discarded those "cute" pieces and the hate verses that did not fit the aesthetic profile she hoped to project. But after rejecting most of her previous work, Dorothy needed more verses to fill the manuscript, so while she was in Europe she briskly churned out nearly forty more pieces, including the raggedly exuberant "Song of Americans Resident in France"[53]— which, as it happened, ultimately did not make the cut. But more than thirty of the new poems did appear in the book.

Enough Rope was released in December 1926. It was both a popular and a personal triumph, for it established, as the *World*'s

---

53. In Paris, Dottie saw but never met the famously reserved James Joyce: "I guess he's afraid he might drop a pearl." The Monte Carlo casino refused to admit her until she was properly dressed: "So I went and found my stockings, and then came back and lost my shirt." Returning home, the transatlantic crossing was "so rough that the only thing I could keep on my stomach was the first mate."

reviewer put it, Dorothy's "secure position as one of the most sparkling wits who express themselves through light verse," with "the higher plane of authentic poetry . . . within her reach." The line that divides light verse and serious "authentic" poetry is an obscure one, and the distinction often hinges more upon the pretentions of the judge than the quality of the work. The road from Nantucket to Xanadu is littered with hopeful submissions. Added the *New York Times*: "Miss Parker's is not society verse in the old sense; it is flapper verse. And as such it is wholesome, engaging, uncorseted and not devoid of grace."

The influence of the book, and its effect upon Dorothy's reputation, ultimately triggered a round of historical revisionism. While the book did sell forty-seven thousand copies, which was a robust performance for a volume of poetry, that level of popularity was by no means as unique as was later assumed. The leading novelists of the time, such as Sinclair Lewis[54] and Edna Ferber,[55] often sold in the hundreds of thousands, and even Samuel Hoffenstein, that other poet signed by Horace Liveright, sold sixty-three thousand copies of his first collection, *Poems in Praise of Practically Nothing*. Yet Samuel Hoffenstein slipped into permanent obscurity—his minor historical footnote derives from his work on the *Wizard of Oz* and *Laura* screenplays—while Dorothy Parker and her work are still objects of broad fascination and steady sales.[56] Dorothy's perspective and expression somehow have resonated through an

---

54. In a New York nightclub a few years later, Dottie overheard the conversation of the next table, a group of visiting midwestern governors: "Sounds like overwritten Sinclair Lewis."

55. Dottie was jealous of Ferber's professional fluidity: "I understand Ferber whistles at her typewriter. And there was that poor sucker Flaubert rolling around on his floor for three days looking for the right words." Because Dottie agonized over every word in her own work, she resented more prolific authors who benefited from America's "proud confusion" of industry and talent: "It is our national joy to mistake for the first-rate, the fecund rate."

56. Dottie: "Yeah, that's me, the toast of two continents—Greenland and Australia."

influential slice of the literary public for more than eighty years, and continue to do so to this day. Perhaps it is the iconoclasm or the calculated irreverence, or perhaps the gaunt and distinctly contemporary candor, but there is something there, particularly in her poems, that draws an audience far beyond what the polite but dismissive reviewers could have imagined.

During the following years she released two more collections of her verses, *Sunset Gun* in 1928 and *Death and Taxes* in 1931, which sold successively fewer copies. Viking Press later compiled the verses from the first three books and, after Dorothy deleted sixteen more items she evidently wanted forgotten, and added five that she had written in the intervening years, issued *Not So Deep as a Well* in 1936.[57] She also published two collections of short fiction, *Laments for the Living,* which received generally positive reviews in 1930, and *After Such Pleasures* in 1933. Viking issued a compilation of the fiction in 1939, with a few new pieces, under the title *Here Lies.* The best of the short stories was "Big Blonde," which was published in Seward Collins's *Bookman* in February 1929, and won the coveted O. Henry competition (and five hundred dollars) for the best short story of that year.

In October 1927, Dorothy finally landed a regular job, and as the *New Yorker*'s book reviewer "Constant Reader," she again delivered more invective than edification.[58] She also assumed

---

57. She dedicated it to Frank Adams, the erudite Comma Hunter of Park Row, who, she once declared, had "raised me from a couplet."

On the subject of couplets, that same year Dorothy supplied one to the Viking Press—by then also her publisher—to promote Adams's compilation, *The Melancholy Lute*; it appeared on its dust jacket and can be found under the title "Blurb" in "The Poems" section of this collection.

58. Dottie later admitted that "it's easier to write about those you hate—just as it's easier to criticize a bad play or a bad book," and some of her most famous cracks appeared in her *New Yorker* column. Dorothy often is credited with these zingers, though without persuasive attribution: "This is not a novel to be tossed aside lightly. It should be thrown with great force." "It was written without fear and without research." And the author who was "a writer for the ages—for the ages four to eight."

Robert Benchley's drama chores after he went to Hollywood, with similar results.[59] She had trouble meeting deadlines,[60] and though the reviews were very popular, they appeared only intermittently between 1928 and 1933, when "Constant Reader" hung up her bookmark permanently.

But Dorothy was sinking deeper into her personal morass. She started a novel, collected an advance, but never finished the book. She had accumulated little money and borrowed constantly from carefully selected friends;[61] she was drinking heavily at the

---

But there were many others that can conclusively be traced to her:

The President's Daughter: Revealing the Love-Secret of President Harding (addressing alleged police attempts to confiscate the printer's plates): "Lady, . . . those weren't policemen; they were critics of literature dressed up."

Lay Sermons, by the author of *The Autobiography of Margot Asquith* "(four volumes, neatly boxed, suitable for throwing purposes)": "The affair between Margot Asquith and Margot Asquith will live as one of the prettiest love stories in all literature"; "This book of essays . . . has all the depth and glitter of a worn dime."

Crude: "It is also a criticism of it." *Shoot If You Must*: "This must be a gift book. That is to say, a book which you wouldn't take on any other terms." *Mistress of Mellyn*: "It is derived from Jane Eyre as painstakingly as a fingerprint is taken from the butt of a gun." *A Matter of Life and Death*: She could not "see eye-to-eye with the one who hailed the book as 'Literature with a capital L.' . . . 'Length with a capital L' is more like it."

Dottie particularly disliked A. A. Milne's "Pooh" books and the cutesy language he affected (a year earlier she had written a nasty verse, "When We Were Very Sore," upon learning that she had been advertised as "America's A. A. Milne," which had caused Robert Benchley to call her "Dottie-the-Pooh"): "And it is that word 'hummy,' my darlings, that marks the first place in *The House at Pooh Corner* at which Tonstant Weader Fwowed up."

59. For example, on Channing Pollack's 1931 play: "*The House Beautiful* is for me the play lousy." Contrary to common belief, she never reviewed *The Lake,* though she may have quipped that Katharine Hepburn "ran the whole gamut of emotion from A to B" as an offhand remark during intermission. She also pretended not to have heard of the star of *The Respectful Prostitute*: "Meg Mundy? What's that, a Welsh holiday?"

60. When the *New Yorker* pressed her for overdue reviews, she was "too fucking busy and vice versa." Her underlying and overriding philosophy: "Work is the province of cattle."

61. In January 1931, "Constant Reader" observed that "when your bank

nearly nightly cocktail parties she both threw and attended,[62] which caused her to run to alcoholic fat and, on occasion, to black out; she also continued to mire herself in hopeless love affairs.[63] She tried to escape her problems by moving, first to The Lowell hotel on the East Side and then to a nearby apartment;[64] and also by traveling, to Hollywood and an MGM studio job for a few

---

account is so overdrawn that it is positively photographic, steps must be taken." Dottie claimed she dreamed of a rural life "raising cheques."

In December 1932, the *New York Herald Tribune* asked her for a list of the ten most beautiful words in the English language. Dottie: "To me the most beautiful word in the English language is cellar-door. Isn't it wonderful? The ones I like, though, are 'cheque' and 'inclosed.'"

62. Dottie's drinking caused even Benchley to suggest that she consider attending Alcoholics Anonymous meetings. After one meeting, she met him at Tony's. Benchley: "Are you going to join?" Dottie: "Certainly not. They want me to stop *now*."

There were many parties, usually involving alcohol, and there were many victims. Dottie professed to despise some partygoers because "their pooled emotions wouldn't fill a teaspoon." Once she was cornered by a conceited young man, the sort she once referred to as "a pony's ass," who talked at her until he advised: "I simply can't bear fools." Dottie: "How odd. Apparently your mother could." At another party, she came across an actor, presumably American, whose season on the London stage had caused him to affect British pronunciation as he repeatedly referred to his "shedule." Dottie: "If you don't mind my saying so, I think you're full of skit." And at another party, their domineering hostess was described as "outspoken." Dottie: "By whom?" At another, she was asked if she had enjoyed herself. Dottie: "Enjoyed it? One more drink and I'd have been under the host."

Other guests eagerly waited for her remarks. At one event a young man actually followed her around before finally admitting: "You're not at all the way I thought you'd be. I'm sorry." Dottie: "That's all right. But do me a favor. When you get home, throw your mother a bone." At another party a woman approached her: "Are you Dorothy Parker?" Dottie: "Yes, do you mind?"

63. In March 1933 she wrote of times "when one had put sex carefully away on the highest cupboard-shelf, in a box marked 'Winter Hats—1916.'"

64. The latter apartment overlooked the East River: "far enough east to plant tea." In a 1928 book review Dottie claimed she wanted to live at "Rising Gorge." Some years earlier she had come up with "Wit's End," which Aleck Woollcott used for his own East Side apartment.

unhappy months in 1928,[65] and to Europe four times between 1926 and 1932.[66] She was particularly depressed and lonely during one European trip, and sent a desperate and entreating letter to a former lover in New York. He replied by telegram—collect: LOVED LETTER DEAR SO HAPPY YOU ARE WELL.

During the spring of 1933,[67] Benchley introduced Dorothy to Alan Campbell, a delicately handsome[68] actor and writer who was eleven years younger than she was. Alan was from Richmond, Virginia, of Scots and Jewish ancestry (his mother[69] was Jewish), whose looks took after his father's side. Although Dorothy was sensitive about the difference in their ages,[70] and there was persistent talk that Alan had engaged in some sort of homosexual activity,[71] they soon

65. On Christmas Day 1928, Frank Adams reported that Dottie had resorted to deception to make new friends: "When the [studio] sign painter arrived to put her name on the door, she bribed him to leave it off and substitute instead the simple legend: 'GENTLEMEN.'"

66. On one occasion, running late as usual, Dottie was shoved on board her departing liner by George Oppenheimer and others. Soon she appeared at the rail: "Guess who's on the boat—Marlene Dietrich! And guess who's not on the boat—my trunk!" Her passage was probably paid by Cross leather-goods heirs Sara and Gerald Murphy, who were living in the Swiss Alps while their tubercular son was undergoing treatment there. Dottie spent much of her trip as their guest, and she bought a lamb coat with "all the warmth and durability of a sheet of toilet paper" to help counter the elements. She sent Frank Adams a postcard: "Sleeping under avalanches. Wish you were with us."

67. Earlier that year, Benchley had told her that former president Calvin Coolidge was dead. Dottie: "How can they tell?" (Decades later, Gertrude Benchley claimed that her husband had replied: "He had an erection.")

68. Dottie referred to him as a "fawn's ass."

69. Dottie claimed her prospective mother-in-law, Hortense Campbell, was a harridan. Some years after the marriage, Dottie and Lillian Hellman were knitting contentedly in front of a roaring fire in the living room while Alan and "Horte" conducted a noisy argument upstairs. Finally Alan stormed down the stairs: "It's as hot as hell in here." Dottie: "Not for orphans."

70. Dottie: "I'm thinking of sending him to military school when he's old enough."

71. Dottie dined in Paris with some lesbians who asked what she thought about same-sex marriage. Dottie: "Of course you must have legal marriages. The children have to be considered." Back at a bar in Greenwich Village a few years

settled into a comfortable routine. Alan was charming and considerate, and he possessed many traits that Dorothy conspicuously lacked, such as frugality, neatness, discipline, and organization. But he also was a pedestrian writer who greatly admired Dorothy's vastly superior talents and reputation. They married in June.[72]

In August 1934 they signed ten-week contracts to write screenplays for Paramount Pictures in Hollywood, at two hundred fifty dollars per week for Alan and one thousand dollars per week for Dorothy. Alan's contract also called for him to act. For several years they earned two thousand dollars a week—for a short time, more than five thousand dollars—and if they claimed to despise both the town[73] and its products,[74] they were, for a while at least,

---

later, Dottie and Alan Campbell were accosted by a customer who appeared flamboyantly gay. He asked if she read fairy tales. Dottie: "My dear, let's not talk shop." She once referred to Campbell as "the wickedest woman in Paris."

As to a notoriously homosexual English actor: "He simply buggers description." And: "Scratch an actor and find an actress."

When Dottie prepared to leave Los Angeles for the last time in 1964, an effete Realtor who lived nearby found some people who were interested in buying her house. While the prospects looked the place over, the neighbor sat with Dottie and basked in her compliments. Finally he left to attend to his customers. Dottie: "There he goes, tossing his little Shirley Temple curls."

72. Dottie was very jealous of other women. When Alan performed in a play, she said the female lead looked like "a two-dollar whore who once commanded five."

73. Dottie praised Budd Schulberg's cutting 1941 novel about Hollywood, *What Makes Sammy Run?*: "I never thought anyone could put Hollywood—the true shittiness of the place—between covers." She once said of a producer: "He hasn't got sense enough to bore assholes in wooden hobbyhorses."

Dottie and Alan spent their honeymoon at George Oppenheimer's in Hollywood while they looked for a house of their own. One Sunday morning Oppenheimer found her examining a publicity photograph in a local newspaper. The circus had arrived in town, and the photo showed three elephants in costume: one wearing a bridal veil, one in a tall silk hat, and the third in a clerical collar. Dottie: "I give it six months."

74. She wired season's greetings to the writer Joe Bryan: IN ORDER TO WISH YOU A MERRY CHRISTMAS I AM INTERRUPTING WORK ON MY SCREEN EPIC, LASSIE GET DOWN.

one of its most popular couples.[75] Yet they left Hollywood[76] with neither fortune[77] nor reputation enhanced.

It is not that the films they wrote were received badly or lost money, but they were generally undistinguished. Though Alan had good work habits and a solid sense of structure, and Dorothy was often superb with dialogue, the results tended to the lackluster. The studio moguls may have possessed banal tastes, but they knew how to produce popular, well-made movies, and they certainly were competent to recognize and reward relative degrees of talent. The former Algonk Donald Ogden Stewart and the occasional Round Table visitor Ben Hecht were

---

75. The writer Louis Adamic attended a summer dinner party wearing a rumpled white cotton suit. Dottie: "Looks like he's come to sell us some leaf tobacco!"

Most of the Los Angeles metropolitan area was still undeveloped when Dottie moved to Hollywood in the mid-thirties. Once she and Aleck Woollcott visited someone who lived on the edge of the wilderness. Their host took them outside to watch wild animals approach the plate of food he had left there. The animals did not appear. They were urged to return, and again they waited, this time until eleven thirty, without luck. Their host was dejected: "Oh, I don't understand it. How could it happen?" Dottie: "I thought we'd at *least* get the after-theatre crowd."

Dottie got along particularly well with John Gilbert, the silent film star whose career had declined sharply when the industry moved to "talkies." She never addressed him as "John" or "Jack"—only "Great Lover of the Silver Screen."

76. At one time Dottie lived in the apartment below George Oppenheimer's in Hollywood. He was notorious for discussing his famous acquaintances. Once she was entertaining some guests when there was a loud crash from above. Dottie was not surprised: "Pay no attention, it's only George Oppenheimer dropping a name."

77. Dottie: "Hollywood money isn't money. It's congealed snow, melts in your hand." She engaged in a joking discussion about burial arrangements with the journalist Vincent Sheean. Dottie: "I want to be buried in a shroud made of unpaid bills from Valentina."

The writer Kyle Crichton asked whether she liked Hollywood. Dottie: "Oh, it's all right. You make a little money and get caught up on your debts. We're up to 1912 now." Yet when a particular producer asked her to write a script, Dottie was offended by his offer: "You can't take it with you, and even if you did, it would probably melt."

A-list writers—Dorothy Parker and Alan Campbell were not.

There was a common misperception at play: that Alan was a Hollywood husband who only worked because he was married to a talented wife.[78] But Alan might have been the better screenwriter of the two and, with his vastly superior work habits, almost certainly was the more valuable asset. Budd Schulberg, the screenwriter and novelist (*What Makes Sammy Run?*) who was closely involved in the events of that time, believed that Dorothy could not have held a job without Alan. When their marriage started to sour, Dorothy tried to prove to Alan that he was the expendable commodity by getting herself fired from *The Pride of the Yankees*. She expected Sam Goldwyn to dismiss Alan, but Goldwyn kept him on the payroll and hired a new writer to replace Dorothy.

The producers may have tended to expect more from Dorothy because they assumed that she was the artist of the partnership but, as the playwright Tom Stoppard observed more than thirty years later, "skill without imagination is craftsmanship," and Dorothy, who never possessed that extraordinary creative spark, ultimately was less an artist than a diligent craftsman. She owed her literary success to a combination of craft, wit, calculated irreverence, and observation—but not artistic vision. She knew how the language worked and how to put words together, and for all the reports of her indolence, she strained to make every single thing she wrote as good as she was capable of doing. "I can't write five words but that I change seven," she once confessed. But writing plays and movies required the imagination to *create* compelling characters and absorbing stories, and that was a quality she lacked. She needed ideas, not craft, and she failed.

During their years in Hollywood, Dorothy and Alan worked for some of the finest producers in the industry, including Goldwyn[79]

---

78. Thea von Harbou tirelessly and tiresomely promoted the career of her husband, the director Fritz Lang. Dottie: "There's a man who got where he is by the sweat of his Frau."

79. The following line has been attributed to Dottie and to several others. In a story conference, Goldwyn, who had once been a glove maker, scolded

and David Selznick, and for a time at the most prestigious studio, Metro–Goldwyn–Mayer.[80] Their screenwriting career peaked when they were nominated for an Academy Award for *A Star Is Born* in 1937, although it is impossible to determine just how much of that film, or any film, they actually wrote, because the studio system of the thirties and forties often assigned a dozen or more writers to one script. Dorothy later claimed that she neither contributed much to the screenplay nor ever saw the completed picture from beginning to end, but she was notoriously and often deliberately inaccurate about such matters. Dorothy and Alan also contributed to the classic *Nothing Sacred,* which was also released in 1937, and Dorothy worked on Alfred Hitchcock's *Saboteur* four years later. (Hitchcock famously inserted himself into one scene in every picture he directed, and in that film Dorothy and Hitchcock played a middle-aged couple driving down a highway.) But the Campbells spent most of their time assigned to forgettable comedies, musicals, and light dramas. Between 1934 and 1949 Dorothy accumulated thirteen screen credits[81] of one sort or another—for "writer," or

---

someone, who retorted: "Don't you point that finger at *me*. I knew it when it had a thimble on it!"

But it was Dottie who responded to Goldwyn's demand that her screenplay end on a happy note: "I know this will come as a shock to you, Mr. Goldwyn, but in all history, which has held billions and billions of human beings, not a single one ever had a happy ending."

80. Dottie had her own version: "Metro–Goldwyn–Merde."

81. She also wrote some impromptu verse in Hollywood, most famously when she sat beside the celebrated English novelist Somerset Maugham at a dinner party thrown by Fanny Brice in early 1941. He recalled she was "demure in black silk, but with a demureness fraught with peril to the unwary."

Maugham once told Dottie that "I am a great admirer of your style." And if Dottie once admitted she felt uncomfortable around Englishmen of a certain class—"whenever I meet one of these Britishers I feel as if I have a papoose on my back"—she managed an elegant response: "Thank you, Mr. Maugham. I have always admired you because you have no style."

Back to Fanny Brice's, a smattering of table talk, and then, as Maugham later recalled, he issued an abrupt challenge: "Why don't you write a poem for me?"

"(original) screenplay," or even for "additional scenes and dialogue."

Dorothy had displayed little interest in either politics[82] or social justice before she joined much of the world in watching the dramatic final appeals of Nicola Sacco and Bartolomeo Vanzetti in 1927. The self-described anarchists had been condemned for two murders near Boston seven years before. For some reason the fate of the two immigrant radicals affected her

---

Dottie agreed and started with the first two lines of a familiar nursery rhyme:

Higgledy Piggledy, my white hen;
She lays eggs for gentlemen.

Maugham told her that the lines had long been among his favorites—though the original nursery rhyme described a *black* hen—and then Dottie completed her rhyme . . . which appears under the title "Pecking Order (or 'Eggs Tempore')" in "The Poems" section of this collection.

But Dottie professed to take offense when she was credited with the verse that ostensibly appeared in the guest book at William Randolph Hearst's San Simeon estate:

Upon my honor
I saw a Madonna
Standing in a niche
Above the door
Of a prominent whore
Of a prominent son of a bitch.

It referred to Hearst and his mistress, the actress Marion Davies. Dottie was appalled that anyone thought she would *ever* resort to rhyming "honor" with "Madonna."

82. Dottie had even warned Heywood Broun against working at the radical and intellectually pretentious *Nation* magazine during the mid-twenties: "You won't be able to hear a thing for the clanking of Phi Beta Kappa keys."

She already had dismissed the fastidiously too-refined tastes of the readers of the other main organ of the left, an affectation evidently epitomized by its editor, Herbert David Croly: "They have a conscious exquisiteness, a deep appreciation of their own culture. They exude an atmosphere of the *New Republic*—a sort of Crolier-than-thou air."

and she jumped into the fray, along with her fellow Algonks Robert Benchley, Heywood Broun, and Ruth Hale. Perhaps her sudden and intense commitment was attributable to Gardner "Pat" Jackson, a handsome Communist fellow-traveler of the familiar physical type. Jackson ran the clemency campaign's Boston office, and that is where Dorothy volunteered to work. Before the anarchists were executed, Dorothy and Ruth Hale were detained by the Boston police in one of the first gentle celebrity political arrests. They were not even fingerprinted[83] before they were released; Dorothy pleaded guilty and was fined five dollars for loitering and sauntering.

Over the ensuing decade Dorothy was increasingly but imperfectly radicalized, and if her conversation occasionally was infected with socialist platitudes, and if she attended a succession of dreary meetings, her normal life continued on its usual path. During the thirties, as the worst sufferings caused by the Great Depression affected great swaths of society, there were new issues and campaigns. In early 1933, Adolf Hitler assumed power in Germany and enacted harshly anti-Semitic legislation. Though Dorothy had never displayed real interest in her Jewish background, Hitler terrified her. In the spring of 1936 she and Donald Ogden Stewart hosted a one-hundred-dollar-a-plate dinner to raise money for what was called the Hollywood Anti-Nazi League.

Stewart was an interesting specimen. He once was a light satirist and humorist even less interested in politics than Dorothy—he had ridiculed her interest in Sacco and Vanzetti—yet he suddenly veered left after he moved to Hollywood and achieved great professional success and remuneration. Stewart was divorced in 1938 by his socialite wife, Beatrice (one of Dorothy's closest friends), who hated his new politics; the next year he married Leonore (Ella) Winter, the attractive Australia-born widow of the muckraker Lincoln Steffens. After the Cold War, a former Communist apparat-

---

83. Though Dottie charged at the time that "they left me a few of theirs. The big stiffs!"

chik claimed that Ella had for several years been "one of the most trusted party agents for the West Coast" when she met Stewart. She was assigned to infiltrate Hollywood and to target people such as Stewart, as she had done with Steffens. Stewart was pleasant and sincere, but he was also a political naïf who was easy prey for some-one like Ella. (But sometimes events play out in unexpected ways: whatever Ella's original intent, it appears she genuinely did fall in love with Stewart, and by all accounts they were devoted to each other until they died three days apart in 1980.)

Some years later, when the Soviet Union was allied with the United States during the Second World War, members of the Hollywood Anti-Nazi League were classified as "Premature Anti-Fascist." And it *was* a Soviet front organization. The speaker at that 1936 dinner was Otto Katz, a Communist propagandist working under an imaginative Stalinist functionary called Willi Münzen-burg, with orders to build Communist influence in the center of world popular culture. Stalin hoped to sway the democracies through the mass media, chiefly by picking at the inadequacies of the capitalist system and its policies. The Depression and the attendant social miseries was one issue. The plight of the Scotts-boro Boys, and the larger issue of racial injustice, was another. The rise of Hitler was a third. The Spanish Civil War, which was, in essence, a battle between surrogates of Hitler and Stalin, was a fourth. Closer to home, the battle to establish an independent writer's union in Hollywood was a fifth.[84]

Though the far left's position on most of these issues was defen-sible, and perhaps even admirable, it also insisted that there was only the single doctrinaire stance on each; it maintained that iso-lated and often transitory problems were invariably "symptoms" of a diseased whole, and that any attempt to explore or to discuss

---

84. A screenwriter dared to tell her that he did not think creative writers belonged in unions. Dottie: "That son of a bitch telling me that *he's* a creative writer? If he's a creative writer, I'm Marie of Rumania!" Dottie even deliv-ered a speech to some cartoonists: "Now, look, baby, 'union' is spelled with *five* letters. It is *not* a four-letter word."

the vastly more severe outrages perpetrated by the Soviet Union against its own citizens, or to compare them with conditions in the democracies, was inherently "fascist."

Katz wanted to recruit people such as Stewart and Dorothy, celebrated artists leading extravagantly luxurious and glamorous lives who wondered whether there was something wrong with that. Ian Hamilton, the author of *Writers in Hollywood, 1915–1951,* noted that they were

> thought of in Hollywood, and elsewhere, as the dandy converts, the pixie revolutionists: New York wisecrackers lured to Hollywood by the big money and now self-politicized in order to assuage their guilt: guilt about writing for films and earning mammoth salaries at the height of the Depression, guilt about having had such a good time during the twenties . . . impressionable and often guilty.

The byzantine corridors of leftist American thought during the thirties were a rat's nest that resists concise explication. But there were three distinct major strains. On its right were the mainstream New Deal liberals, who usually supported Franklin D. Roosevelt and most of the existing economic and social order, but who believed that some reforms were essential for it to survive. This group included Robert Benchley and most of the literary class. To their left were the democratic socialists, who supported parts of the present system and were basically patriotic, but who also suspected the profit motive and what they saw as the untrammeled power of the plutocrats. This group included Heywood Broun and most of the rest of the literati.

On the far left were the embattled Trotskyites, who followed the deposed Leon Trotsky, and the Stalinists, usually so described by their opponents. The Stalinists presumed to support various high-minded policies that promised to lead to the socialist utopia of equality, prosperity, and peace, but, as Edmund Wilson put it in a May 1944 *New Yorker* review, Dorothy succumbed to the expiatory mania that has become epidemic with film writers and was presently making earnest appeals on behalf of those organizations which talked about being "progressive" and succeeded in convincing their followers that they were working for social revolution, though they had really no other purpose than to promote the foreign policy of Stalin.

Dorothy not only backed the left's correct position on the "easy" issues, and even dressed the part by affecting a dowdy proletarian look around chic Hollywood, but she also supported the vastly less popular and defensible Stalinist line on two key issues that arose later in the decade. First, she signed a petition that endorsed the verdicts that were handed down from the notorious show trials that accompanied the Great Purge of 1936–38, during which Stalin put millions of his own people to death. This murderous campaign caused most previously loyal Communists and fellow travelers to denounce Stalin and to move to the right, but not Dorothy.

And then, in August 1939, Stalin signed the infamous non-aggression pact with Hitler, which caused virtually all of the remaining independent hard left to abandon Stalin publicly. But when the leaders of the Hollywood Anti-Nazi League, including Dorothy, heard of the agreement, they leaped into action—and immediately renamed themselves the Hollywood League for Democratic Action, presumably to avoid offending their new allies. Some of Dorothy's supporters have claimed that she was chagrined by the Soviet–Nazi alliance, but there is no contemporaneous evidence of it. In fact, she refused to criticize it publicly, even though she had been moved to radicalism partly because of the West's lukewarm response to Hitler's Jew-baiting policies.

While it is not certain whether Dorothy formally joined the Communist Party, she probably did. She publicly declared herself to be a Communist in 1934 (though there was a tinge of adolescent grandiosity to the statement), and she invoked her

Fifth Amendment right against self-incrimination when she was specifically asked about it twenty years later. But it is clear that despite her emotional sentimentality, her intellectual incoherence, and the utter lack of discipline that characterized, inter alia, her flirtation with the revolutionary struggle, she was by any reasonable definition a Stalinist. Stephen Koch, who has written extensively on the subject, observed that "Parker's union of style and Stalinist attitudes was a natural fit. Through the chic of her hard-left commitments, Parker could both validate her love of glamour, and mask it with an appropriate look of disdain for all the vanities." And according to Bea Stewart, Dorothy "was not a personal friend of the multitudes. She was a very, very *grande dame,* and contrariness was the wellspring of her communism. She was anti. She was anti the Establishment."

If Communism purported to help humanity, then she was, in her own simplistic, romantic way, a Communist, and dialectic be damned. Some apologists later excused her actions because she meant well, a useful defense that is routinely employed by erstwhile radicals, but seldom afforded to even the most repentant former reactionaries. But even if Dorothy's intent *was* pure, which is doubtful, she still condoned, and outspokenly supported, and even helped to finance the brutal policies of a hostile and genocidal regime. If she wasn't a scoundrel, she was a fool. Pick one.

Dorothy's excursion through the hard left cost her many friendships,[85] most notably Robert Benchley's, and her viciously ad hominem intolerance for opposing views caused her to cut loose from most of her remaining longstanding relationships, including those with Bea Stewart and Sara and Gerald Murphy. It ultimately put her name near the top of some of the blacklists that circulated through the industry[86] and effectively destroyed

---

85. She tended to hector, as when advising a presumably astigmatic political moderate: "Stop looking at the world through rose-colored bifocals."

86. While she was blacklisted in the late forties, a drunk harassed her at a bar. Dottie: "With the crown of thorns I wear, why should I be bothered with a prick like you?"

what remained of her screenwriting career, but she never wavered and even attracted a new confidante, with Svengalian overtones, along the way.

Lillian Hellman was a gifted playwright and a doctrinaire Stalinist (though she also would have disputed the label) who was twelve years younger than Dorothy. They forged a close friendship in the mid-thirties, shortly after Hellman broke into the popular consciousness before her thirtieth birthday with the remarkable success (nearly seven hundred Broadway performances) of her first produced play, *The Children's Hour*. Perhaps it was Hellman's success at such a young age, in a field that Dorothy had so dearly hoped to conquer herself, that led Dorothy to ascribe some greater insight or comprehension to her than Hellman in fact merited. Whatever the reason, Hellman quickly gained, and jealously guarded, an intellectual and emotional influence over Dorothy that endured through the final thirty years of Dorothy's life.

Dorothy also admired Hellman's lover, the writer Dashiell Hammett,[87] though Hammett intensely disliked Dorothy. Hammett was even more radical than Hellman: for example, as German bombers battered the United Kingdom during the Battle of Britain in 1940—a year before Hitler negated the 1939 nonaggression pact by attacking the Soviet Union—Hammett led a Stalinist Hollywood front organization whose sole function was to disrupt British efforts to obtain American aid. It was called, with the sneering vulgarity of the True Believer Thug, the "The-Yanks-Are-Not-Coming-Committee." (Before the United States entered the First World War, George M. Cohan had promised the embattled Allies that "the Yanks are coming" in his stirring anthem "Over There.") It was probably Hellman, with surreptitious help from Hammett, who molded Dorothy's

---

87. Dottie, in a rare critical remark about her physically unattractive friend: "The trouble with Lillian Hellman is she thinks she's Dashiell Hammett—when she only looks like him."

increasingly extreme politics during the late thirties and helped to maintain it through the forties.

Meanwhile, the poetry compilation *Not So Deep as a Well* went through five printings and comprised the greater part of the more than thirty thousand dollars in royalties that Dorothy earned between 1935 and 1937. But the Campbells, and particularly Dorothy, often spent more than they made, and in 1936 they splurged on the Fox House, a colonial farmhouse and barn on more than one hundred acres near Doylestown in scenic Bucks County, Pennsylvania, north of Philadelphia. They paid less than five thousand dollars for it, but then spent ninety-eight thousand dollars to renovate and landscape the property.[88] They shuttled between Hollywood and Bucks County until Alan enlisted in the Army Air Force in 1942, and they eventually sold the farm in 1947—for forty thousand dollars.[89]

They sold it because they were getting divorced. The first years of the marriage were happy enough, and Dorothy was uncharacteristically civil to her new husband until she suffered two miscarriages, first in 1936 and again in 1939,[90] the latter

---

88. Several other writers who lived nearby were incensed when Dottie and Alan cut down some trees on the property. Dottie: "Fifty-second Street Thoreaus."

89. The columnist Leonard Lyons asked her to describe the property in two words. Dottie: "Want it?"

90. Dottie's maternal instincts were not finely honed. Harold Guinzburg's son Thomas once overheard her say: "Oh, my, if only the Guinzburg children were as well behaved as the Guinzburg dogs." (Harold Guinzburg and George Oppenheimer had founded the Viking Press in 1925. Guinzburg bought Oppenheimer's share eight years later.)

She was fascinated by Joe Bryan's six-year-old son, John, and his ability to get very dirty very quickly, "without seeming to try." Dottie: "I could take John into 21 and leave him at the center table while I went to the ladies' room for no more than a moment, and when I came back, he'd be covered with *tar*!" Bryan recalled the time, during the forties, when Dottie entertained his young children with "the little-known fable" of Aesop and the Wolf: "Well, Aesop was walking through this forest one day, when he came upon a great big wolf caught in a trap. The wolf begged him, 'Please, nice Mr. Aesop, one quickly followed by a hysterectomy. Some psychological alchemy caused Dorothy to release her anger by viciously turning on Alan. She gained a lot of weight—Gertrude Benchley claimed Dorothy considered having a breast-reduction operation in the late thirties—and increased her drinking even further, causing Alan also to drink excessively to keep up with her. She enjoyed humiliating him publicly, often by accusing him of a fondness for young men, just as nearly twenty years before she had publicly accused Eddie Parker of drug addiction. After Pearl Harbor she insisted that Alan enlist and was inordinately pleased when he enrolled as a private, as one of the masses, in the Army Air Force. When he applied for officer's training school, she tried to sabotage his application.[91]

Alan ultimately was promoted to captain and served with Army Air Force intelligence, first in London and later in Paris. Dorothy turned fifty in 1943.[92] She was fat, and after the barrels of Scotch whiskey and gallons of martinis and cases of chain-smoked Chesterfield cigarettes,[93] she appeared much older than

---

help me out of this cruel trap!' So Aesop did, and when the wolf was free, he bit Aesop on the ankle and said, 'Now go write a fable about *that*!'"

91. Dottie visited Alan in Miami Beach when he graduated from officer's training school in 1942. The Broadway director Joshua Logan also attended the school. Dottie told Logan she was thirsty. Logan went hunting but came up dry, so he offered her a bottle of Coca-Cola, a beverage that Dottie insisted she had never tasted before. After she had a few sips, Logan asked if she felt better. "No, but as it was going down I learned a deep, abiding truth about drinking Coca-Cola." What was that? "Never send a boy on a man's errand."

92. At a dinner party during the war, Dottie approached a woman of about her own age, but who was dressed and acting like a giddy debutante as she fussed over a clearly uncomfortable army colonel. The woman turned to Dottie: "It's his uniform; I just love soldiers."

Dottie: "Yes, you have in every war."

Another time a catty socialite approached Dottie: "Don't you think that dress is a little young on you, darling?" Dottie: "Perhaps. Yours looks lovely on you—but then again, it always does."

93. One time Dottie dropped her cigarette lighter and it bounced under the sofa. Joe Bryan's knees cracked when he kneeled to retrieve it. Dottie

she was. The quality of her fiction had deteriorated as her political radicalization progressed; she inserted ham-handed diatribes into much of her work, and the best editors, including Harold Ross,[94] grew leery of publishing her. In 1939 Alan and Dorothy wrote a play called *The Happiest Man,* but it was too polemical to be produced commercially. In 1944 she wrote her last published verse, a weird piece that forgave soldiers for wartime adultery. It appeared in the *New Yorker.*

Dorothy told several friends that she also wanted to contribute to the war effort. Perhaps her application to join the Women's Army Corps was denied because of her age, and perhaps she was not allowed a war correspondent's credential because the government would not issue her a passport due to her subversive background, but perhaps not. Meanwhile, her collected fiction was rereleased by Modern Library, and an anthology[95] of her work was selected by Aleck Woollcott as the fourth in a series of volumes intended for soldiers overseas. It was released stateside by Viking in 1944 as *The Portable Dorothy Parker.*[96] Of the original ten volumes in Woollcott's series, only three have remained in print continuously through the ever-evolving tastes of the past sixty-five years: the Bible, the Shakespeare, and the Parker.

But Dorothy wanted to do more. She delivered speeches and raised funds for government-issued War Bonds and the USO. (The "United Service Organizations" provided support for the troops.) And at the July 1943 convention of the Emergency Conference to Save the Jews of Europe, she passionately promoted

smiled, rubbed her hands together, and extended them toward Bryan: "Ah, there's nothing like an open fire—!"

94. There was one particularly stormy argument. Dottie: "When the revolution comes, it will be everybody in the world against Harold Ross!"

95. Dottie did not like anthologists: they were sluggards who liked a comfortable evening at home "raiding a good book."

96. She was living in New York again. In 1945, someone asked why she was hanging around the Viking Press office. Dottie: "Witting for my publisher again." Once she watched Diana and Vincent Sheean's infant daughter toddle through a park: "Isn't it a pity she never married?"

a scheme to evacuate four million European Jews to Turkey.

While the campaign for European Jewry was a vital cause, it emphasized the ambivalence with which she always had regarded her Jewish background. The trauma of her school years had taught her how much of the world regarded Jews. Her usual response had been to obscure her ancestry, which is why some of her acquaintances said that her only happy reminder of her first marriage was the classically Anglo-Saxon surname that allowed her to be "Mrs. Parker." If later in life she would coyly claim that "I was just a little Jewish girl trying to be cute,"[97] she also could write an anti-Semitic poem, "The Dark Girl's Rhyme," in 1926, when she was earning her reputation. In the thirties she had discovered a new god, the deity of radical social-ism, which she still served, yet in the midst of a war that nearly destroyed the world's Jewry, she stood in active support of their survival. Yet in later years, when Jewish survival of another sort was at stake in the State of Israel, she displayed no interest.

It would be unfair to conclude that her sudden concern for the Jews during the war was at all insincere, but she soon reverted to more familiar causes, raising funds for children's books as a member of the National Council of American-Soviet Friendship in 1944, and assuming the acting chairmanship of the Spanish Ref-ugee Appeal, another "anti-fascist" front organization, in 1945.

At the war's end Alan wrote to tell Dorothy that he was involved with another woman; the liaison did not endure but he returned home in late 1946 to a dead marriage. While the details of the legal skirmishing that ensued are unclear, they divorced in Las Vegas in May 1947.[98]

For most of the three years she was divorced from Alan,

97. Near the end of her life, she reluctantly refused to write her autobi-ography, despite several offers. Dottie: "I'd like to write the damned thing, just so I could call it *Mongrel!*"

98. After the divorce, Vincent Sheean told Dottie he felt sympathy for Alan. Dottie: "Oh, don't worry about Alan. Alan will always land on some-body's feet."

Dorothy was entangled with Ross Evans, a vastly inferior version of the familiar type.[99] Evans was a radio announcer and an alcoholic, more than twenty years younger than Dorothy. He moved into her apartment at a New York hotel and became her writing partner, despite possessing no talent discernible to anyone else. "They" wrote magazine articles and then a play called *The Coast of Illyria,* which failed, predictably. But about the same time Dorothy cowrote the story, though not the shooting script, for the hit movie *Smash-Up: The Story of a Woman.* Dorothy's story of a woman who married a future radio star and later fell into alcoholism earned her an Academy Award nomination and a writing deal with Twentieth Century–Fox for herself and Evans. After returning to Hollywood she was told to reduce her drinking,[100] but Evans liked the bottle and eventually deserted her for another woman. And he stole her dog, or so she claimed.

Dorothy remarried Alan Campbell three months later, in August 1950.[101] Dorothy cut her hair short and lost most of her excess weight, and the reconciliation appeared to go well for several months, but then the anticommunist investigations that were gaining momentum put Alan in danger of being blacklisted. He blamed Dorothy for involving him in radical politics during the thirties—against his better judgment, as he recalled it. There were nasty fights, and less than a year after remarrying they had separated again.

Dorothy had attacked the House Un-American Activities

99. As Dottie and Evans left a party, a friend of hers complimented his tan. Dottie: "Ah, yes. He has the hue of availability."

100. Evans: "One of her doctors said he didn't like her kidneys and she later confessed that she didn't like his nose." Not surprising: at Joe Bryan's in 1949, he asked what she wanted for breakfast. Dottie: "Just something light and easy to fix. How about a dear little whiskey sour?"

101. Dottie coyly pulled the sheet over her face when they awakened the morning of the day of their second marriage: "Mustn't see the bride before the wedding." And at the reception after the wedding: "People who haven't talked to each other in years are on speaking terms again today—including the bride and groom."

Committee (HUAC) during the late forties, and she was often threatened with subpoena, but her 1951 encounter with FBI agents was vastly more sinister. They asked about her ties to the Communist Party, which she denied had ever existed.[102] In truth, though she still occasionally talked the radical talk, her political fires had largely sputtered out years earlier[103] on every issue but civil rights. Nonetheless, in 1951 HUAC cited Dorothy and three hundred other writers, artists, actors, and professors for affiliating with Communist front organizations. Ultimately, however, Dorothy escaped official punishment.

Others were not so lucky during the fifteen anxious years that followed the Second World War. Though self-promoters and fanatics such as the congressmen Martin Dies, Jr., and J. Parnell Thomas perpetrated outrages in pursuit of their antisubversive "investigations," it is also true that many of their targets were or had been Communists, and some had conspired to insert Soviet propaganda into Hollywood films. Lillian Hellman managed to escape punishment through some seemingly courageous testimony—actually it was cleverly deceptive—but Hammett and many others were sent to prison, and some, such as Ella and Donald Ogden Stewart, fled to Britain or other countries. Accusations that Dorothy was either a dangerous Communist or merely a subversive dupe effectively destroyed what remained of her Hollywood career. She was informally blacklisted through most of the fifties.

In mid-1952, Dorothy was thrilled to move back to New York and the Volney Hotel on East Seventy-fourth Street. The Volney and similar hotels in good Upper East Side neighborhoods housed a large number of older women living alone, so Dorothy and a

---

102. A federal agent asked whether she had conspired to overthrow the United States government. Dottie: "Listen, I can't even get my dog to stay down. Do I look to you like someone who could overthrow the government?"

103. She discussed the thirties more than twenty years later: "They were progressive days. We thought we were going to make the world better—I forget why we thought it, but we did."

younger playwright called Arnaud d'Usseau[104] sat down to write a play about those women and their lonely lives. As Dorothy was old, and lonely, she was writing about herself again. They called it *Ladies of the Corridor,* but it was too gloomy to succeed. The director, Harold Clurman, suggested cutting a character who committed suicide, which would have allowed a happy ending, but Dorothy refused. The play opened in October 1953 to mixed but decent reviews. The critic George Jean Nathan called it the best play of the year, but it closed after six weeks.

Dorothy was writing short fiction again for the *New Yorker,*[105] and in 1957 she started writing book reviews for *Esquire* for six hundred dollars per month. Over the next five years she wrote forty-six book review columns and one short story for the magazine. *Esquire*'s publisher, Arnold Gingrich,[106] paid her whether she submitted her column or not—her work habits had not improved—and even raised her salary to seven hundred and fifty dollars per month. She took it because she was sixty-five and had no money. Other projects were considered but later dropped. She wrote one song lyric for the 1956 Leonard Bernstein operetta *Candide.* It failed.

By then Dorothy had reached the age when elderly celebrities often were honored for not having died yet,[107] generally by

---

104. Dottie met Kate and Zero Mostel through d'Usseau. They played Botticelli, a role-reversal game where the "it" player had to deduce an identity through clues given in a question. Dottie's stumper question: "Do you chase men for business and pleasure?" Answer: J. Edgar Hoover.

105. Though Dottie admitted in 1963 that she seldom read the magazine anymore: "It always seems to be the same old story about somebody's childhood in Pakistan."

106. At a dinner, Gingrich was describing himself as "just a simple country boy from Michigan" when he heard the murmur. Dottie: "When convenient."

107. Dottie sat next to the African-American leader W. E. B. Du Bois at his ninety-second birthday celebration in 1960. Some African spear-dancers performed in front of them and, in the course of the dance, thrust their spears increasingly closer to the honoree. Dottie leaned over to Du Bois: "Watch out, mate, or you'll never see ninety-three."

obscure organizations intending to burnish their own reputations through the glory reflected by their honorees. She fielded requests from people who wanted to hear about the Round Table and the literary twenties. She made recordings and gave readings of her works; she agreed to interviews that allowed her to continue to wage the campaign against the Table and its era that she had started twenty years earlier when she moved to the left. Of the decade, she admitted: "Damn it, it *was* the twenties and we had to be smarty. I *wanted* to be cute."[108] The Table "was no Mermaid Tavern, I can tell you. Just a bunch of loudmouths showing off, saving their gags for days, waiting for a chance to spring them." In any case, "the only one with any stature who came to the Round Table was Heywood Broun"—the only leftist among them at the time—and that one quickly tired of "their little jokes all about themselves." Her comments about George S. Kaufman were mixed, verging on incoherent: he was (1) "a nuisance and rather disagreeable"; though (2) "I guess he was sort of funny"; but (3) "whoever claimed that he ever said anything funny?"; and (4) he did not "even know what satire is." Kaufman, she concluded, was "a mess."

In early 1961, Dorothy reluctantly reconciled with Alan, again,[109] and they returned to Los Angeles to work for Charlie Brackett (who had written the Algonquin roman à clef *Entirely Surrounded* more than a quarter-century before) at Twentieth Century–Fox. They lived in Alan's small West Hollywood bungalow on a one-block street called Norma Place. It was a close-knit community where they grew friendly with their neighbor Wyatt Cooper,[110] a screenwriter in his early thirties, later the

---

108. Later in the same interview, Dottie said: "There's a helluva distance between wisecracking and wit. Wit has truth in it; wisecracking is simply calisthenics with words."

109. Though still jealous, she doubted Alan was sleeping with a notably reserved acquaintance. Dottie: "I know you aren't laying her. If you were, you'd have splinters in your prow."

110. Dottie's tongue never mellowed, even into old age. Cooper recalled

father of the television journalist Anderson Cooper (who was born the week Dorothy died).

Dorothy was fired when she failed to appear for work regularly. The Campbells survived on unemployment insurance, on occasional payments for television licenses to her old short stories, and on the cash Alan raised by hawking Dorothy's review books, at least until she finally quit the *Esquire* job at the end of 1962. Dorothy also delivered a few lectures and taught two courses as a celebrity instructor at Los Angeles State College, an experiment that ended badly.

Meanwhile, she and Alan were again drinking heavily and were again at each other's throats. That is, they were until June 14, 1963, when Dorothy found Alan dead in a little hideaway den he had built for himself. He was fifty-nine. The official cause of death was an overdose of the barbiturate Seconal. Alan's body was found with a plastic dry-cleaning bag draped around his head and shoulders, so it was listed as a probable suicide; nonetheless, Dorothy and some friends maintained the death was accidental.[111] Dorothy did not attend the funeral.

----

how she referred to a woman with a rasping tone: "Doesn't she have the loveliest voice?" Or the way she "flattered" an actor whose huge nose emphasized his lack of a perceptible chin: "Oh, they've been *searching* for a new Cary Grant." (The man actually believed her.)

A narcissistic neighbor sustained a small scratch on her face in an auto accident: "I did hope there wouldn't be a scar." Dottie: "As opposed to all those women who *like* looking like they went to school at Heidelberg."

Several celebrities lived in the neighborhood, including the actress Estelle Winwood. Dottie reacted strongly when she was told that Miss Winwood was appearing in the play *Camelot*: "Playing a battlement, no doubt."

Another neighbor commissioned a huge painting of himself—with full and detailed frontal nudity. Dottie: "It's so real, you almost feel he could speak to you, don't you?"

111. When Alan's body was taken away, Dottie was approached by a woman she did not like, identified in one account as June (Mrs. Oscar) Levant. In overly effusive terms, the woman asked how she could help. Dottie: "Get me a new husband."

After a second of shocked silence, the woman sputtered: "I think that is

Dorothy turned seventy[112] two months later. She grew increasingly infirm, with several serious medical problems, and was nearly blind without her glasses. She returned to New York and the Volney.[113] From there she shuttled in and out of hospitals,[114] and hired a private nurse for several months. She could not control her alcoholism: in a thinly fictionalized 1976 *Esquire* piece, Truman Capote[115] wrote that "Dottie has been such a lush—you'd never know when her face is going to end up in the soup."

Someone suggested she draw up her will, and she bequeathed her estate, which primarily consisted of her copyrights, to Martin Luther King, Jr., and upon his death to the National Association for the Advancement of Colored People (NAACP). Dorothy had never met Dr. King, but she greatly admired him nonetheless, and the bequest conformed with her stance on the cause that had long been most important to her: civil rights.

Although Bea Stewart was again her most trusted friend, Dorothy appointed Lillian Hellman executor of her estate. Bea spent

the most callous and disgusting remark I ever heard in my life." Dottie: "So sorry. Then run down to the corner and get me a ham and cheese on rye and tell them to hold the mayo."

112. Dottie is reported to have said two things on that birthday: "Promise me I shall never grow old." And: "If I had any decency, I'd be dead. Most of my friends are."

113. Her apartment was quite small: "Yes, it's tiny. But you wouldn't believe how expensive it is. You would think it was built for an elephant. And not a pink one."

114. During one of her hospital stays, a doctor warned that if she did not stop drinking she would be dead within a month. Dottie sighed: "Promises, promises."

115. Truman Capote and Tallulah Bankhead attended the dinner party where Dottie met the actor Montgomery Clift, who was widely rumored to be homosexual. Capote recalled the scene: "'He's so beautiful,' murmured Miss Parker. 'Sensitive. So finely made. The most beautiful young man I've ever seen. What a pity he's a cock sucker.' Then, sweetly, wide-eyed with little-girl naïveté, she said: 'Oh. Oh, dear. Have I said something wrong? I mean, he is a cock sucker, isn't he, Tallulah?'"

Bankhead: "Well, d-d-darling, I r-r-really wouldn't know. He's never sucked my cock."

much of her time trying to raise money upon which Dorothy could live, while Dorothy got into the habit of taking whatever royalty and other checks that were sent her, some for sizable amounts, and stuffing them into drawers, often unopened. She also reestablished her friendship with Sara Murphy.

In 1965, as Dorothy's health improved, she started to circulate publicly.[116] Wyatt Cooper and his socialite wife, Gloria Vanderbilt Cooper,[117] also had moved to New York, and he resumed his friendship with Dorothy. And if Dorothy was warily fascinated with society, the sentiment was reciprocated: perhaps she professed distaste about it, but she still scrupulously followed the activities of its leaders[118]—who, as it turned out, were eager to meet her. She was delighted when, in March 1967, the Coopers threw an elegant dinner party in her honor that was attended by much of *tout* New York.[119]

During the afternoon of June 7, 1967, Dorothy suffered a fatal coronary in her Volney apartment. She was seventy-three. The next day the news of her death was reported on the front page and nearly a full jump page of the *New York Times*. Her body was cremated and, after her ashes went unclaimed, they were stored in her attorney's file cabinet for more than twenty years.

Dorothy left a net estate of slightly more than twenty thousand dollars. The murder of Dr. King less than a year after Dorothy's death should have terminated Hellman's executor authority once she transferred the estate to Dorothy's ultimate

---

116. Dottie took a young man to see a mid-sixties too-contemporary play titled *Luv*. After five minutes she turned to him: "I have a feeling you're going to *like* this." And they left.

117. Dottie made sport of Gloria's social position, calling her "Gloria the Vth."

118. Dottie heard that the famous transsexual Christine Jorgensen lived on Long Island with her mother. Dottie: "And what sex, may I ask, is the mother?"

119. At the Cooper party, a guest admired the wineglasses: "I always think that wine tastes so much better in lovely glasses, don't you?" Dottie: "Oh, yes. Paper cups aren't right."

legatee, the NAACP, but Hellman vigorously defended her right to milk Dorothy's estate, without any discernible legal grounds to do so. Hellman publicly fumed that "that goddamn bitch" had betrayed her by not leaving Hellman the income from Dorothy's copyrights for the remainder of Hellman's life (she died in 1984). According to Hellman, Dorothy ostensibly had promised to do so because Hellman had supported Dorothy through the last years of Dorothy's life. In fact, Hellman had helped with some matters but had not, by any means, subsidized Dorothy; moreover, during those last years Hellman had avoided Dorothy whenever she could manage to do so. Hellman later was exposed as a chronic liar of memorable proportions.

In 1972, a court ordered Hellman to turn the estate over to the NAACP, but in an interview with Nora Ephron[120] the next year Hellman argued, with astonishing presumption, that her legal stance should have been vindicated because of her superior political virtue: "It's one thing to have real feeling for black people, but to have the kind of blind sentimentality about the NAACP, a group so conservative that even many blacks now don't have any respect for, is something else. She must have been drunk when she did it. I was executor, you know."

In a letter he drafted a few weeks after Dorothy's death, the eminent *NewYorker* writer E. B. White assigned Dorothy Parker's professional legacy: "Seen in perspective, though, some of the well-loved figures of those days have shrunk with the passage of time. Dotty Parker died on Page 1, but except for a handful of sterling short stories her contribution to letters was slight and she herself knew that she was not much of a poet."

---

120. Nora Ephron's screenwriter parents, Phoebe and Henry Ephron, socialized with Dottie in Hollywood. Once Dottie was at their house for a game of anagrams. The writer Sam Láuren came up with "currie." Dottie insisted there was no such word. Phoebe Ephron settled the dispute with a jar of Crosse and Blackwell "currie" powder. Dottie: "What do they know? Look at the way they spell Crosse."

Yet, as the English poet W. H. Auden astutely observed, "some books are undeservedly forgotten, none are undeservedly remembered." Evidently Aleck Woollcott saw something the others missed when he offered this prediction in that essay he collected in 1934, "Our Mrs. Parker":

> I do suspect that another generation will not share the con-
> fusion into which Mrs. Parker's poetry throws so many of
> her contemporaries, who, seeing that much of it is witty,
> dismiss it patronizingly as "light" verse, and do not see that
> some of it is thrilling poetry of a piercing and rueful beauty.

For ultimately we must address that simple question: why is Dorothy Parker so peculiarly memorable? Why do her poems stay in print, decade after decade, when the reputations of so many of her critically preferred contemporaries, even "serious" poets such as Edna St. Vincent Millay and Elinor Wylie, have faded with time? Is it another symptom of an insidious vulgarization of High Culture, or is it something else? Though merit and popularity clearly are distinguishable qualities, are they also contradictory? Could it be that her work is just that much better than the "experts" have ever been willing to recognize?

More than forty years have passed since Dorothy Parker's death. In that time she has been instated as a sort of minor but resilient historical figure, largely literary but not exclusively so, known for a time and a taste but not for one thing in particular. In a 1995 *Commentary* magazine essay, the critic Hilton Kramer supplied a useful accounting for the architect Philip Johnson; perhaps the appraisal also applies to Dorothy—but perhaps not:

> There are certain figures in the arts who, although minor in
> accomplishment and equivocal in their aesthetic influence,
> are so completely representative of the spirit of their age
> that they come to occupy a historical position far greater
> than the intrinsic merits of their work could ever justify.

By one count, no fewer than thirty discrete editions of Dorothy's work have been published in the United States, and Dorothy has also been the subject of dozens of newspaper and magazine articles, five book-length biographies, an eponymic period murder mystery, a feature film, a postage stamp, and hundreds of entries in quotation and anecdote collections, which may cumulatively act to keep us interested, but not to make us aware. In an affectionate 1968 *Esquire* profile of Dorothy, Wyatt Cooper concluded: "If you didn't know Dorothy Parker, whatever you think she was like, she wasn't. Even if you did know her, whatever you thought she was like, she probably wasn't." And that is that.

Dorothy wrote more than 330 poems and free verses in the thirty years from 1915 to 1945. She published nearly three hundred of these during the twenties, an average of more than one poem or free verse every two weeks. It was a prolific achievement but for her a matter of economic survival, because the poems and free verses were a primary source of income during the seven years between her dismissal from *Vanity Fair* in 1920 and her appointment as the *New Yorker*'s "Constant Reader" in 1927.

Dorothy originally published these poems and free verses in at least twelve newspapers and magazines: first in *Vanity Fair* (1915–19, 1926) and *Vogue* (1916); then in *Life* (1920–27), the *Saturday Evening Post* (1922–23); Frank Adams's "The Conning Tower" in the *World* (1923–31), and the *New York Herald Tribune* (1931–35); the *New Yorker* (1925–44); and the *Bookman* (1927–28). She also published single pieces in the *New Republic* and *McCall's* (both in 1927), and the *Yale Review* (1930); another appeared in the collaborative book *Nonsenseorship* (1922); she even wrote a rhyme for a Simon & Schuster advertisement that appeared in the *Saturday Review of Literature* in 1931, and a couplet promoting Frank Adams's *The Melancholy Lute* in 1936. Most of her pieces appeared in *Life* (130), "The Conning Tower" (70), the *New Yorker* (60), *Vanity Fair* (22), and the *Saturday Evening Post* (19). She was probably paid for all of them except the "Conning Tower" pieces, the unpublished items, the Frank Adams blurb, and likely also the *Nonsenseorship* piece; she collected most of them—more than two hundred in all—in her three books of original poetry and two subsequent compilations. Of the remainder, 121 poems and free verses—almost all the forgotten ones—were collected for the first time in the original edition of *Not Much Fun* in 1996. Four more items are collected in this new edition for the first time. Also appearing here for the first time in any compilation is the full text of Dorothy's poem "The Passionate Screenwriter to His Love"; a small part of it—about one-fourth—appeared in the original edition of *Not Much Fun*.

Some of the scholars who studied Dorothy Parker have referred to these "lost" pieces; a few have even extracted from them. But the vastly greater proportion of these works did not appear in print after their original publication in those newspapers, magazines, and books from 1915 to 1938; that is, until the publication of these two editions of *Not Much Fun*. Some of the biographers have speculated about why Dorothy did not include these pieces in her earlier collections. They tend to conclude that she was embarrassed by some of her earlier and implicitly inferior work. The publisher of one of her compilations delicately suggested that she had not included "some" verses from her earlier collections because they were "no longer to her taste."

There is some truth to that. The earlier works are, on the whole, more lighthearted and ephemeral. They tend to be more exuberant, and to possess less artistic merit. But Dorothy also employed other criteria for her selections—and rejections. Recall that she was trying to project a certain image (even retitling and editing many of her poems before collecting them), and many of her earlier works undermined that pretense. It appears she was not allowed to collect any of the nineteen poems she had published in the *Saturday Evening Post,* which retained its copyrights. One account has it that Dorothy was blackballed by that magazine after she publicly ridiculed some friends of the publisher George Horace Lorimer, and perhaps years later there was a desire to retaliate further by refusing her permission to reprint. And perhaps some of the previously uncollected items evoked unpleasant or embarrassing memories that were better left undisturbed; pieces like "A Musical Comedy Thought," with its whiff of improper appropriation; and "Pollyanna Gets the Air," and its reminiscence of the Charles MacArthur affair; and "To Elspeth," with its vulgar tinge of refuted envy.

But whatever Dorothy's motivations may have been, there is reason to appreciate the work she chose to leave behind. It is more eclectic. It is breezier. And it is vastly less self-conscious. Most of these pieces appeared during the early to mid-twenties, a hectic time when Dorothy often submitted a poem nearly every week, which forced her to cast around for ideas wherever she could find them. Some of the pieces dissected current fads, such as in the slang-spewing "Invictus" or "The Passionate Freudian to his Love"; some profiled current celebrities, such as "Lynn Fontanne" or "*Life*'s Valentines"; others marked various annual celebrations, such as "Christmas, 1921" or "Paging Saint Patrick." Some were more personal and explored subjects that ranged from her love of animals ("To My Dog"), to her precarious financial situation ("Song for the First of the Month"), to what was becoming her particular obsession, the perils of evanescent love ("Lyric" and particularly "Pollyanna Gets the Air").

These previously uncollected pieces also contain nearly all of Dorothy's experiments in structured poetic forms, including her first triolet (a short poem with a rhyme scheme of *ab, aa, abab*; with the first line repeated as the fourth and seventh lines, and the second line repeated as the eighth); sonnet (a fourteen-line poem, usually in iambic pentameter, that fully expresses a single thought or sentiment in either of two rhyme schemes: she preferred the Italian, with an octave followed by a sestet, to the English, with three quatrains followed by a couplet); and ballade (usually a three-stanza poem with identical rhyme schemes, followed by an envoi, and with each of the stanzas and the envoi having the same final line). She also attempted the rondeau (a ten- or thirteen-line poem on two rhymes, with the opening words repeated twice as unrhymed refrains).

Dorothy gloried in new language and was, in her own way, an important historical resource. In her very first poem, "Any Porch" (September 1915), she referred to Irene Castle's "bobbed hair"; in May 1919's Our Office hate verse, she exulted that "the sky's the limit"; but, as she warns in the October 1918 Bohemians hate verse, she does not "mess around"; even as she admitted in a February 1928 *New Yorker* review that she was a "bird-brain." As the twenty-five-year-old critic reminisced in *Vanity Fair* in January 1919, "those were the days." According to the most authoritative reference, the *Oxford English Dictionary*, in each instance Dorothy's is the first known use of the word or phrase. And there are many more. . . .

The hate verses are a particularly rich and amusing source of contemporaneous references. For example, in her harangue against Slackers, which was published in the heady days of late 1917, when the United States was officially in the First World War but not yet really bloodied by it, Dorothy the war bride indicted the Conscientious Objectors, whom she judged "the real German atrocities," and the Pacifists, who "will do anything on earth to have peace / Except go out and win it"; but in an ironic anticipation of her own destiny, she also ridiculed the Socialists, "The Professional Bad Sports" who "don't want anybody to have any fun." (Less than a year later, in her diatribe against Bohemians, she attacked "The Table D'Hôte Bolsheviki. / They are always in revolt about something. / Nothing has been done yet that they can wholly approve of.")

In her June 1921 tirade against Parties, she fulminated against obnoxious card players before she warned that "they shoot men like Elwell." Joseph Bowne Elwell, the so-called Wizard of Whist, was a noted bridge authority and skirt-chaser shot dead the previous year in a classic "locked room" murder mystery. (In 1926 this publisher, Scribner, published *The Benson Murder*

Case, the first installment of the celebrated "Philo Vance" detective series by "S. S. Van Dine," the pen name of Willard Huntington Wright. *Benson* is a roman à clef of the Elwell affair.)

Later in 1921, in that scrutiny of Movies, Dorothy reflected the New York litterateur's emerging envy of Hollywood salaries, when she described the star Hollywood actress who "supports an indulgent husband / In the style to which he has become accustomed; / The wages of sin is $3,500 a week." Twelve years later she met Alan Campbell. . . .

Those precarious undertakings called "art" are considered and judged through intensely personal yet hazy prisms of emotion, taste, and experience. This collection will ultimately be measured on those grounds. Enjoy.

The
Poems

(And Some "Modernist Verse")

THE BRIDGE FIEND

How do we cut for the deal?
        That's so, we did it before.
Partner, we'll beat them, I feel—
        Oh, I just hate keeping score!
Really, I don't understand,
        Under the line or above?
Partner, just *look* at my hand!
        I must be lucky at love.

Partner, I haven't a thing—
        The hearts were dealt in a lump.
Don't tell me that was *your* king—
        Well, then, I've wasted a trump.
Now it's my bid, I suppose—
        Goodness, who dealt me this mess?
You made it lilies on *those*?
        Isn't it time to progress!

Oh, did you see what you did?
        Why, you're an absolute dub!
Didn't you hear what I bid?
        Couldn't you lead me a club?
Kindly keep track of what's played—
        What a remarkable lead!
Tell me how many we made—
        Set us three hundred? Indeed!

ANY PORCH

"I'm reading that new thing of Locke's—
   So whimsical, isn't he? Yes—"
"My dear, have you seen those new smocks?
   They're nightgowns—no more, and no less."

"I don't call Mrs. Brown *bad*,
   She's *un*-moral, dear, not *im*moral—"
"Well, really, it makes me so mad
   To think what I paid for that coral!"

"My husband says, often, 'Elise,
   You feel things too deeply, you do—'"
"Yes, forty a month, if you please,
   Oh, servants impose on *me*, too."

"I don't want the vote for myself,
   But women with property, dear—"
"I think the poor girl's on the shelf,
   She's talking about her 'career.'"

"This war's such a frightful affair,
   I know for a fact, that in France —"
"I love Mrs. Castle's bobbed hair;
   They say that *he* taught her to dance."

"I've heard I was psychic, before,
   To think that you saw it—how funny—"
"Why, he must be sixty, or more,
   I told you she'd marry for money!"

"I really look thinner, you say?
        I've lost all my hips? Oh, you're *sweet*—"
"Imagine the city to-day!
        Humidity's *much* worse than heat!"

"You never could guess, from my face,
        The bundle of nerves that I am—"
"If you had led off with your ace,
        They'd never have gotten that slam."

"So she's got the children? That's true;
        The fault was most certainly his—"
"You know the de Peysters? You *do*?
        My *dear*, what a small world this is!"

THE GUNMAN AND THE DÉBUTANTE
A Moral Tale

A wild and wicked gunman—one who held a gang in thrall—
    A menace to the lives of me and you,
Was counting up, exultingly, the day's successful haul—
    As gunmen are extremely apt to do.
A string of pearls, a watch or two, a roll of bills, a ring,
    Some pocketbooks—about a dozen, say—
An emerald tiara—oh, a very pretty thing!
    Yes, really, quite a gratifying day.

A dainty little débutante came trippingly along,
    With wistful, trusting eyes of baby blue;
She softly hummed a fragment of a most Parisian song—
    As débutantes are very apt to do.
That wild and wicked gunman felt he couldn't miss the chance
    To end his busy day triumphantly;
"Though scarcely in the habit of attacking débutantes,
    Your money or your life, my dear," said he.

The dainty little débutante was trembling with alarm,
    Appealingly she looked him through and through,
And laid her helpless little hand upon his brawny arm—
    As débutantes are very apt to do.
Then earnestly she prayed the wicked gunman to be good,
    She begged that he'd reform that very day;
Until he dropped his wicked gun, and promised that he would,
    And bade her go her sweet and harmless way.

The wild and wicked gunman sat considering it all.
      "At last," he cried, "I've met my Waterloo";
He vowed he'd give to charity the day's successful haul—
      As gunmen are extremely apt to do.
But when he tried to find his gains and give to those in want—
      The pocketbooks, the watches, bills and ring—
He found, to his amazement, that the little débutante
      Had taken every solitary thing!

THE LADY IN BACK

I don't know what her name is, for you see we've never met;
       I don't know if she's dark, or if she's fair;
I don't know if she's young or old, or rich or poor—and yet
       Whatever place I chance to go, she's there.
I don't know where she came from, and I don't know where she'll go;
       Why fate has linked our lives I cannot see,
The world's so full of people—oh, I'd really like to know
       Why must she *always* sit in back of me?

She's always right on duty when I go to see a play—
       Unfailingly, she's seen that play before,
And so she tells what's coming, in her entertaining way—
       For me, the drama holds surprise no more.
"Now watch, the husband enters, as I told you that he would,
       At first you'll think he'll shoot her, but he'll not.
And later she goes back to him, and says that she'll be good"—
       Obligingly she thus unfolds the plot.

When I am at the opera, of course she's sure to come.
       She there adopts another policy—
The more familiar arias she feels obliged to hum,
       And always just a trifle off the key.
But when the singers reach those heights to which she can not climb—
       Oh, then I plumb the very depths of gloom!
For, lest I be too happy, she will occupy that time
       By long accounts of who's in love with whom.

I never can avoid her at the humble picture show,
   Of course, the film is always one she's seen
Reliable as Mary's lamb, she's right behind, I know,
   Revealing all the secrets of the screen.
When heroes tumble over cliffs, as movie heroes will,
   And villains blow up bridges, just for fun,
I know that she takes pleasure in extinguishing my thrill
   By telling just exactly how it's done.

I really couldn't tell you if she's widow, maid, or wife;
   I've never heard about her family;
I don't know who appointed her to take the joy from life,
   I can't imagine what she sees in me.
I often sit and think of it, and wonder why it's so,
   Why, every place that I am, she is too,
The whole wide world to choose from—oh, I'd really like to know
   Why can't she *sometimes* sit in back of you?

OH, LOOK—I CAN DO IT, TOO

Showing That Anyone Can Write Modernist Verse

Bacchanale

Hand in hand, we ran through the Autumn forest;
Our laughter soaring on the wings of the mad wind;
In and out, tracing a fantastic path,
Through the passionate, flaming dogwood
And the slim, virginal birches,
Our limbs flashing white against the riotous background.
The grape-leaves I twined rested lightly on your hair,
And, as we ran, you shouted snatches of wild songs—
Pagan hymns of praise to the dead gods.
On we rushed, dizzy with the strong wine of Autumn. . . .
I wonder if you were married, too.

Sunday

A litter of newspapers
Piled in smothering profusion.
Supplements sprawling shamelessly open,
Flaunting their lurid contents—
"Divorced Seven Times, Will Re-Wed First Wife,"
And, "Favorite's Account of Escape from the Harem."
Unopened sheets of "help" advertisements;
Editorials, crumpled in a frenzy of ennui;
Society pages, black with lying photographs.
Endless, beginningless heaps of newspapers. . . .
Outside, a thin gray rain,
Falling, falling hopelessly,
With a dull monotony of meaningless sound,
Like the voice of a minister reading the marriage service.

The Picture Gallery

My life is like a picture gallery,
With narrow aisles wherein the spectators may walk.
The pictures themselves are hung to the best advantage;
So that the good ones draw immediate attention.
Now and then, one is so cleverly hung,
That, though it seems unobtrusive,
It catches the most flattering light.
Even the daubs are shown so skillfully
That the shadows soften them into beauty. . . .
My life is like a picture gallery,
With a few pictures turned discreetly to the wall.

Fragment

We came face to face in the crowd;
Hemmed all about by pushing, straining figures,
Berserk with the thought of getting home to dinner.
Heavy about us rose the odor of crowded humanity,
Hot in our ears sounded their polyglot curses.
But the crowd was kind, for it pushed you into my arms,
There you rested, one supreme moment,
Your delicate body quivering with exquisite timidity.
We stood, we two alone, on the pinnacle of rapture,
Our souls throbbing together.
Then we were torn apart.
But Hope leaped high within me,
For, before you were borne away from me,
You whispered a few shy syllables—
The answer to my feverish question. . . .
Why did you give me the wrong telephone number?

LETTER TO ROBERT BENCHLEY

Roughing It in the Country at The Birches, Maine

Greetings to all from the pine-scented woods!
We hope everybody is feeling so good.
Kindly forgive our writing in pencil;
It's too much trouble to get the other utensil.
We want to tell you about this place.
With us it certainly stands like an ace.
To-day we went out on the lake to fish;
That you were with us, was our heartiest wish.
We caught a trout, not to mention some chubbs,
And then put them back, like a couple of dubs.
A salmon then got on the line by mistake,
But we put him back, for the little ones' sake.
The lake at times is fairly rough.
We go out upon it, though.
The water is cold and full of salmon,
And the scenery hereabouts is charming.
Our Septoline has given out—
We're better off, there's not a doubt.
But still, we'd like a dash of hootch,
In fact, we'd like it very much.
As yet, we have not been in bathing,
We're waiting for a warmer occasion.
We're saving our bathing-suits, crisp and new,
To give to some Ziegfeld ingenue.
The trail around the island's fine;
To-day we saw some porcupines.
The tennis court is a perfect whale;
We thought at first it was part of the trail.
The Wallace Frye just broke a shaft—
You should have heard the captain laugh!
Some children here have the whooping-cough.
If we don't get it, we'll be in soft.

The desk clerk's manner is proud and airy,
Nevertheless, we think he's a fairy.
There are some people right next door
Who turned out to be a terrible bore.
There always seems to be some kind of a hitch
Isn't Nature a (finish this line for yourself, and
  get a year's subscription to the Boston Post.)
The captain's trousers may be out at the seat;
But he stands ace-high with Mr. Bradstreet.
He should worry about cash in hand,
He's got a rating of 800 *thousand*.
Each time the boat sails, he's on her
To collect 54 cents from each passenger.
We expect to be back on Sunday noon,
Or if not then, some fine day soon.
We'll return to the city, 'mid sighs and tears,
With vacation over for another year.
We're feeling fine—the same to you,
And now it's late, we must say adieu.
We think of you all, on the Biltmore roof
And wish you were with us, that's the God's truth.
We watch the flickering firelight,
And wonder if Duggie and Robby are tight.
In the firelight glow, so cheery and warm,
We weep over the mortgage on the Benchley farm.
And now we cannot write any more,
So, once again, we must say au revoir.

OUR OWN HOME TALENT

Miss Isadora Quigley pays
      Terpsichore devotion;
In rhythmic bliss, she bends and sways—
      The true *vers libre* of motion.
She blithely bounds o'er field and stream,
      Attired with Greek simplicity,
And gives, the while, her basic scheme
      A lot of free publicity.
Her genius is, as all agree
      Who watch her do her dances,
An infinite capacity
      For taking awful chances.

You may not care for it—but there!
It keeps her in the open air.

The name of Mr. Eustace Young,
      Our author, sharp and Shavian,
Some day will be on every tongue—
      Including Scandinavian.
He has, he's often told, a *flair*
      For tense and throbbing crudity;
On every page his soul lies bare,
      In literary nudity.
Already he is hailed as great
      By cultural minorities,
For all his works have been, to date,
      Suppressed by the authorities.

Our *literati* have confessed
Nothing succeeds like the suppressed.

Now art Miss Iris Blount employs;
       Her batik and her stencil
Express her maiden griefs and joys,
       She swings a wicked pencil!
In forms of cube and octagon,
       Ignoring technicalities,
She splashes her impressions on,
       In broadest generalities.
She paints no view of moonlit glen,
       No landscape, green and grassy;
Her subjects run to gentlemen
       And ladies, in their chassis.

Her art, our connoisseurs imply,
Is all in the beholder's eye.

To down all kings and presidents
       Our Mr. Tench proposes;
His loudly uttered sentiments
       Are redder than the roses.
He urges anarchism's cause
       In terms concise, but notable;
And what he says about the laws
       Would scarcely pass as quotable.
He pleads that marriages be few,
       While love be free, in plenty—
Which last endears him greatly to
       The local *cognoscenti*.

His word is law, among our set,
On rules of sovietiquette.

WITH BEST WISHES

Glad Christmas Day once more has come—
       There's little novelty in that.
It's welcomed eagerly by some,
       Which isn't to be marveled at.
Their stockings hold a house and lot
       (I hope you gather what I mean),
A picturesquely furnished yacht.
       A next year's model limousine,
A sable wrap of graceful cut,
       A sheaf of cheques for vast amounts;
It's not the thought that matters, but
       The gift which goes with it that counts.

But I'LL get a multitude of seasonable cards,
       A bowl full of lily bulbs, approaching their decease;
A pair of gilded shoe-trees, with appropriate regards,
       And a leather-bound "Evangeline," with colored frontispiece.

It's scarcely any wonder that
       The season finds me all unmoved,
For Father Christmas leaves me flat—
       Step-Father Christmas, it has proved.
'Twas ever thus—from early youth
       I've seen my hopes decay, because
Too soon I learned the bitter truth:
       There isn't any Santa Claus.
Each Yuletide mocks my touching trust;
       The give and let give is my plea,
It's Christmas Day for some, but just
       December twenty-fifth for me.

For I'LL get a paper-weight, to crush my Christmas cheer,
A hand-painted needle-case, a brace of button-hooks,
A host of cordial wishes for a prosperous new year,
And a holiday edition of the "Rubaiyat," de luxe.

I've often heard that some there are—
    How hard such tales are to believe!
To prove that costlier by far
    It is to give than to receive.
On Christmas they present their friends
    With motor cars, and pearls in strings,
And blocks of stock with dividends,
    And other useful little things.
Though I have no such benefits,
    I sing the Christmas spirit's praise.
I know the giver's thrill—for it's
    A poor Yule which won't work both ways.

So I'LL give a laundry bag, of chintz refined, yet gay;
A tooth-brush container of a fanciful design,
A flock of timely greetings for a snappy Christmas Day,
And a highly colored copy of "That Old Sweetheart of Mine."

INVICTUS

Farthest am I from perfection's heights,
        Faulty am I as I well could be,
Still I insist on my share of rights.
        When I am dead, think this of me:
Though I have uttered the words "Yea, bo,"
        Though I use "ain't" to get a laugh,
Though I am wont to explain "Let's go,"
        Though I say "You don't know the half"—
Black through my record as darkest jet,
        Give me, I beg, my devil's due;
Only remember, I've never yet
        Said, "How's the world been treating you?"

"What could be sweeter?" I fondly muse;
        "You said a mouthful," I confess;
Witnesses testify that I use
        "Yes, indeedy," in times of stress;
"Oh, it's a great life," I loudly claim—
        "If you don't weaken," I amend;
"I'll tell the world," is my middle name;
        "Well, how's the boy?" I greet a friend.
While I acknowledge each grave defect,
        Still I am master of my fate—
All that I ask you is, Recollect
        I never said, "I'm here to state."

"Yours till hell freezes," I sign my mail;
      "I'll say it is," I coyly cry;
"What's the good word?" is my cheery hail;
      Bidding farewell, I say "Bye-bye";
I demand, "How do you get that way?"
      "Oh, have a heart," is all my plea;
Speaking of oysters, I sadly say,
      "I like them, but they don't like me."

Humbly I own to each one of these,
      Yet I atone for all my slips;
Heap me a measure of credit, please—
      "Kiddie" has never passed my lips.

A MUSICAL COMEDY THOUGHT

My heart is fairly melting at the thought of Julian Eltinge;
    His vice versa, Vesta Tilley, too.
Our language is so dexterous, let us call them ambi-sexterous—
    Why hasn't this occurred before to you?

SONG OF THE OPEN COUNTRY

When lights are low, and the day has died,
I sit and dream of the countryside.

Where sky meets earth at the meadow's end,
    I dream of a clean and wind-swept space
Where each tall tree is a stanch old friend,
    And each frail bud turns a trusting face.
A purling brook, with each purl a pray'r,
    To the bending grass its secret tells;
While, softly borne on the scented air,
    Comes the far-off chime of chapel bells.
A tiny cottage I seem to see,
    In its quaint old garden set apart;
And a Sabbath calm steals over me,
    While peace dwells deep in my brooding heart.

And I thank whatever gods look down
That I am living right here in town.

THE PASSIONATE FREUDIAN TO HIS LOVE

Only name the day, and we'll fly away
    In the face of old traditions,
To a sheltered spot, by the world forgot,
    Where we'll park our inhibitions.
Come and gaze in eyes where the lovelight lies
    As it psychoanalyzes,
And when once you glean what your fantasies mean
    Life will hold no more surprises.
When you've told your love what you're thinking of
    Things will be much more informal;
Through a sunlit land we'll go hand-in-hand,
    Drifting gently back to normal.

While the pale moon gleams, we will dream sweet dreams,
    And I'll win your admiration,
For it's only fair to admit I'm there
    With a mean interpretation.
In the sunrise glow we will whisper low
    Of the scenes our dreams have painted,
And when you're advised what they symbolized
    We'll begin to feel acquainted.
So we'll gaily float in a slumber boat
    Where subconscious waves dash wildly;
In the stars' soft light, we will say good-night—
    And "good-night!" will put it mildly.

Our desires shall be from repressions free—
      As it's only right to treat them.
To your ego's whims I will sing sweet hymns,
      And *ad libido* repeat them.
With your hand in mine, idly we'll recline
      Amid bowers of neuroses,
While the sun seeks rest in the great red west
      We will sit and match psychoses.
So come dwell a while on that distant isle
      In the brilliant tropic weather;
Where a Freud in need is a Freud indeed,
      We'll be always Jung together.

LOVE SONG

Suppose we two were cast away
          On some deserted strand,
Where in the breeze the palm trees sway—
          A sunlit wonderland;
Where never human footstep fell,
          Where tropic love-birds woo,
Like Eve and Adam we could dwell,
          In paradise, for two.
Would you, I wonder, tire of me
          As sunny days went by,
And would you welcome joyously
          A steamer? . . . So would I.

Suppose we sought bucolic ways
          And led the simple life,
Away—as runs the happy phrase—
          From cities' toil and strife.
There you and I could live alone,
          And share our hopes and fears.
A small-town Darby and his Joan,
          We'd face the quiet years.
I wonder, would you ever learn
          My charms could pall on you,
And would you let your fancy turn
          To others? . . . I would, too.

Between us two (suppose once more)
   Had rolled the bounding deep;
You journeyed to a foreign shore,
   And left me here to weep.
I wonder if you'd be the same,
   Though we were far apart,
And if you'd always bear my name
   Engraved upon your heart.
Or would you bask in other smiles,
   And, charmed by novelty,
Forget the one so many miles
   Away? . . . That goes for me.

IDYL

Think of the things that can never come true—
        Save in the shadowy country of dreams.
Think of what might be, for me and for you,
        Could we but shatter the world's sorry schemes.
Think of our own little vine-covered nest;
        Each day, at sunset, I'd wait for you there,
Down by the gate, in the glow of the west,
        Dressed all in white, with a rose in my hair.

Think of a chair, softly-cushioned and wide;
        Think of a hearth, where the red firelight dies;
Think of me sitting there, close by your side,
        Reading the stories writ deep in your eyes.
Think of the years, like an unending song,
        Think of a quiet we never have known.
While, all forgotten, the world rolls along,
        Think of us two, in a world of our own.

Now that you've thought of it seriously—
Isn't it great that it never can be?

ABSENCE

I never thought that heav'n would lose its blue
     And sullen storm-clouds mask the gentle sky;
I never thought the rose's velvet hue
     Would pale and sicken, though we said good-by.
I never dreamed the lark would hush its note
     As day succeeded ever-drearier day,
Nor knew the song that swelled the robin's throat
     Would fade to silence, when you went away.

I never knew the sun's irradiant beams
     Upon the brooding earth no more would shine,
Nor thought that only in my mocking dreams
     Would happiness that once I knew be mine.
I never thought the slim moon, mournfully,
     Would shroud her pallid self in murky night.
Dear heart, I never thought these things would be—
     I never thought they would, and I was right.

TO MY DOG

I often wonder why on earth
        You rate yourself so highly;
A shameless parasite, from birth
        You've lived the life of Reilly.
No claims to fame distinguish you;
        Your talents are not many;
You're constantly unfaithful to
        Your better self—if any.
Yet you believe, with faith profound,
        The world revolves around you;
May I point out, it staggered 'round
        For centuries without you?

In beauty, you're convinced you lead,
        While others only follow.
You think you look like Wallace Reid,
        Or, at the least, Apollo.
The fatal charms with which you're blest,
        You fancy, spell perfection;
The notion, may I not suggest,
        Is open to correction?
An alien streak your tail betrays;
        Your ears aren't what they would be;
Your mother was—forgive the phrase—
        No better than she should be.

One can but feel your gaiety
        Is somewhat over-hearty;
You take it on yourself to be
        The life of every party.
In bearing, while no doubt sincere,
        You're frankly too informal.
And mentally, I sometimes fear,
        You're slightly under normal.
The least attention turns your brain,
        Repressions slip their tether;
Pray spare your friends the nervous strain
        And pull yourself together!

You take no thought for others' good
        In all your daily dealings,
I ask you, as a mother would,
        Where *are* your finer feelings?
I think I've seldom run across
        A life so far from lawful;
Your manners are a total loss,
        Your morals, something awful.
Perhaps you'll ask, as many do,
        What I endure your thrall for?
'Twas ever thus—it's such as you
        That women always fall for.

LYRIC

How the arrogant iris would wither and fade
      If the soft summer dew never fell.
And the timid arbutus that hides in the shade
      Would no longer make fragrant the dell!
All the silver-flecked fishes would languish and die
      Were it not for the foam-spangled streams;
Little brooks could not flow, without rain from the sky;
      Nor a poet get on without dreams.

If the blossoms refused their pale honey, the bees
      Must in idleness hunger and pine;
While the moss cannot live, when it's torn from the trees,
      Nor the waxen-globed mistletoe twine.
Were it not for the sunshine, the birds wouldn't sing,
      And the heavens would never be blue.
But of all Nature's works, the most wonderful thing
      Is how well I get on without you.

FULFILMENT

I do not sit and sigh for wealth untold,
      It never thrusts itself into my schemes;
I shrink from all your piles of clanking gold—
      Better my sparkling hoard of golden dreams.
A life of limousined and jeweled ease
      Is but a round of fathomless *ennui*.
Your motor cars, your pearls, your sables—these
      Are naught to me.

Better a homely flat in Harlem's wilds
      Than a costly living's spurious benefits;
Better a simple butter-cake at Childs'
      Than caviar and stalled ox at the Ritz.
Your unearned gold, to me, is shot with flaws;
      A life of honest toil I'd make my lot—
Which really makes it very nice, because
      It's what I've got.

SONG FOR THE FIRST OF THE MONTH

Money cannot fill our needs,
       Bags of gold have little worth:
Thoughtful ways and kindly deeds
       Make a heaven here on earth.
Riches do not always score,
       Loving words are better far.
Just one helpful act is more
       Than a gaudy motor car.
Happy thoughts contentment bring
       Crabbed millionaires can't know;
Money doesn't mean a thing—
       Try to tell the butcher so!

None can stretch his life an hour
       Though he offer boundless wealth:
Money, spite of all its pow'r,
       Cannot purchase ruddy health.
Simple pleasures are the best,
       Riches bring but misery,
Homely hearts are happiest,
       Joy laughs loud at poverty.
Pity those in Mammon's thrall,
       Poor, misguided souls are they,
Money's nothing, after all—
       Make the grocer think that way!

Greatest minds the world has known
      All agree that gold is dross
Man can't live by wealth alone;
      Bank books are a total loss.
Banish strife and greed and gloom,
      Throw off money's harsh control,
Sow good deeds, and watch them bloom—
      Hyacinths, to feed the soul.
Hoard no pelf, lest moth and rust
      Do their work and leave you flat.
Money? It is less than dust—
      Laugh the landlord off with that!

LYNN FONTANNE

Dulcy, take our gratitude,
      All your words are gold ones.
Mistress of the platitude,
      Queen of all the old ones.
You, at last, are something new
      'Neath the theatre's dome. I'd
Mention to the cosmos, you
      Swing a wicked bromide.

Heroines we've known, to date,
      Scattered scintillations
(Courtesy the Wilde estate)
      Through their conversations.
Polished line and sparkling jest—
      They've provided plenty.
Dulcy's bromides brought us rest—
      Dulcy far niente.

TO MARJORIE RAMBEAU

In "Daddy's Gone A-Hunting"

If all the tears you shed so lavishly
       Were gathered, as they left each brimming eye.
And were collected in a crystal sea,
       The envious ocean would curl up and dry—
So awful in its mightiness, that lake,
       So fathomless, that clear and salty deep.
For, oh, it seems your gentle heart must break,
       To see you weep.

We try to tell ourselves it isn't true,
       We strive to feel that dawn must follow dark,
We strain to hold the thought that, off-stage, you
       Are happy as the widely-mentioned lark.
But, though you wring our feelings to their cores,
       Our devastated hearts you seem to keep,
For, oh, we pack the theatre to its doors
       To see you weep.

CHRISTMAS, 1921

I do not ask you for presents rare,
        Other-world trove of forgotten metals;
Orchids that opened to jungle air,
        Tropical hate in their writhing petals;
Onyx and ebony, black as pain,
        Carved with a patience beyond believing;
Perfumes, to harry the startled brain;
        Laces that women have died in weaving;
Cool-tinted pearls from the ocean, where
        Grottoes of dolorous green regret them.
I do not ask you for presents rare—
        Dearest, I know that I wouldn't get them.

Give me your love, on this Christmas Day.
        Give me your thoughts, when the chimes are ringing.
Send me the happier along my way,
        Deep in my soul let your words be singing.
Give me your wishes, as bells sound clear,
        Charming the air with their golden measure.
Give me your hopes for the unborn year,
        Fill up my heart with a secret treasure.
Give me the things that you long to say,
        All of your tenderest dreams unfetter.
Give me your love, on this Christmas Day—
        But come across, please, when times get better.

MARILYN MILLER

From the alley's gloom and chill
      Up to fame danced *Sally*.
Which was nice for her, but still
      Rough upon the alley.
How it must regret her wiles.
      All her ways and glances.
Now the theatre owns her smiles,
      Sallies, songs, and dances.

Ever onward *Sally* goes—
      Life's one thing that's certain.
O'er the end of other shows
      Let us draw a curtain.
Their untimely ends are sad,
      But they stood no chances,
For, you see, they never had
      Sally's songs and dances.

FRAGMENT

Why should we set these hearts of ours above
>   The rest, and cramp them in possession's clutch?
Poor things, we gasp and strain to capture love,
>   And in our hands, it powders at our touch.
We turn the fragrant pages of the past,
>   Mournful with scent of passion's faded flow'rs,
On every one we read, "Love cannot last"—
>   So how could ours?

It is the quest that thrills, and not the gain,
>   The mad pursuit, and not the cornering:
Love caught is but a drop of April rain,
>   But bloom upon the moth's translucent wing.
Why should you dare to hope that you and I
>   Could make love's fitful flash a lasting flame?
Still, if you think it's only fair to try—
>   Well, I am game.

FIGURES IN POPULAR LITERATURE

THE SHEIK

The desert chieftain here behold,
    The Dempsey of the Nile.
He knocks the lady readers cold
    And cramps their husbands' style.
The heroine reels back for more.
    They play like happy kids—
He tells his love, then knocks her for
    A row of pyramids.

She revels in his gallant deeds;
    Her passions higher mount
Each time he languidly proceeds
    To drop her for the count.
They marry in the end—they do
    In all such compositions—
And now, no doubt, he'll knock her through
    Another twelve editions.

So if you'd knock the ladies dead,
Just use your right and go ahead.

THE FLAPPER

The playful flapper here we see,
    The fairest of the fair.
She's not what Grandma used to be—
    You might say, *au contraire*.

Her girlish ways may make a stir,
   Her manners cause a scene,
But there is no more harm in her
   Than in a submarine.

She nightly knocks for many a goal
   The usual dancing men.
Her speed is great, but her control
   Is something else again.
All spotlights focus on her pranks,
   All tongues her prowess herald,
For which she may well tender thanks
   To God and Scott Fitzgerald.

Her golden rule is plain enough—
Just get them young and treat them rough.

THE DRAB HEROINE

There was a time, as doubtless you're
   Enabled to recall,
When heroines of literature
   Were not like this at all.
Their hair was heaped in glinting curls,
   Their forms were wondrous fair,
And when it came to sex, the girls
   Admittedly were there.

To-day, toward woolen lingerie
   The lady's thoughts are turned,
And sex is in its infancy
   So far as she's concerned.

A kitchen drudge, whom all ignore,
   She leads a life entrancing
As Cinderella's was, before
   She took up ballroom dancing.

Abandon hope, and learn to cook,
And you will figure in a book.

THE WESTERN HERO

This hero ranks among the best—
   He's Nature's rugged child.
You've heard about the woolly West?
   'Twas he who drove it wild.
Observe that he is dressed to kill
   (Forgive the pun, I pray),
In pranks like this he finds a thrill—
   He's simply full of play.

In his revolver terrors lurk;
   His aim's a deadly one.
Could Annie Oakley see his work,
   She'd throw away her gun.
He trifles not with woman's love,
   In spite of his virility,
For he's a charter member of
   The natural nobility.

He shoots to kill and aims to please;
Our books are filled with such as these.

THE GLAD GIRL

This child of curious tendencies
        To your acquaintance add.
Her smile is permanent, for she's
        The gladdest of the glad.
Come battle, famine, flood, or fire,
        The cheery little one
Accepts it as her heart's desire,
        And says, "Ain't we got fun?"

The joy of living fills her cup;
        Of hope, she's never rid.
Imagine how she'd brighten up
        Your household—God forbid!
The bitter ills her fortunes send
        She sprinkles smiles galore on;
It seems to me our little friend
        Is something of a moron.

But if I had her author's pelf,
I'm sure that I'd be glad, myself.

THE BOY SAVANT

Behold, in all his native state,
        Dispensing truths profound,
The gifted undergraduate,
        The learned campus hound.
His reading fills his youthful head
        With thoughts that throb and hum,
For Nietzsche, as is often said,
        Abhors a vacuum.

In lighter moments, he's the man
        That fills the flappers' dreams;
He'd make the All-American—
        If there were petting teams.
His self-regard is scarcely small,
        His conversation shows it;
Just ask him anything at all—
        For he's the boy that knows it.

Oh, youth verbose, our feelings spare—
For God, for country, and forbear!

THE GREAT LOVER

I'm sure you've met this lad before;
        His work is fast, though rough.
He feels that all is fair in war—
        In love, it's fair enough.
His tale the Vice-Suppressor takes,
        And drinks in every word
(A single swallow never makes
        A Sumner, we have heard).

Our hero lived in ages gone—
        The days of bright romance.
We read about his goings-on
        And sigh, "So this is France!"
You must concede, the boy was good
        Among the local ladies;
But his intentions toward them would
        Not pave the streets of Hades.

How sweet to read of days of old
When knights, to say the least, were bold!

CHANTEY

A wet sheet and a straining sail,
     And a sea of shifting blue;
A wide sky and a rousing gale,
     And joy in the heart of you;
A clean line, where the sky hangs low
     And a seagull soars and dips;
And the old voice that bids men go—
     Go down to the sea in ships.

So go and sail the gold sea, the bold sea, the cold sea;
     The waving, craving, raving sea that's fringed with silken
       foam;
Oh, go and sail the green sea, the keen sea, the mean sea—
     But if it's all the same to you, I'll stick around at home.

The swift turn of the night-wind's whim,
     And the tang of hempen strings;
The sharp snap of the halyards slim,
     And the spray that cuts and stings.
The wild chorus the breezes hum,
     And the waves that prowl and creep;
And the old voice that bids men come—
     Come over the tameless deep.

So go and sail the white sea, the light sea, the bright sea,
     The dashing, crashing, smashing sea, that dances in the gale;
Go on and sail the sad sea, the bad sea, the mad sea—
     But if it's just the same to you, I'd rather be in jail.

MORAL TALES FOR THE YOUNG [1]

Maude, the brightest of the sex,
Forged her daddy's name to checks,
Took them to the local banks,
Cashed them, with a smile of thanks.
All the money came in handy—
Maudie was so fond of candy!
Weight she gained in way affrighting,
So she's given up her writing.

Save the money, when you forge;
Little ladies do not gorge.

Don, the little apple-cheek,
Sold his aunt's blue-ribbon Peke,
Sneaked it out of Auntie's house,
Hidden in his sailor blouse.
Donald planned to spend his earnings
Gratifying all his yearnings.
But the chance for pleasure slipped him,
For the doggie's buyer gypped him.

If they can't complete the deal,
Nicer children do not steal.

LIFE'S VALENTINES

PRINCESS MARY AND VISCOUNT LASCELLES

Here behold, and likewise lo,
Princess Mary and her beau.
Bright her cheek with maiden blush;
Shall we say a royal flush?
How we've watched their love's ascents
In the Sunday supplements!
Blessings for the happy pair;
For their photographs—the air!

MR. DAVID WARK GRIFFITH

Look, and you will surely find
Right above, the Master Mind.
(Just a nickname of his own
Which he worked up all alone.)
He it was who made, they say,
Movies what they are to-day;
This the goal for which he's tried—
Lord, I hope he's satisfied!

DAVID BELASCO

Often in the local press
On your kindness you lay stress.
Love's the basis of your art,
So you say—that is, in part.
Frequently you tell us of
How devotedly you love
Actors, public, critics, too . . .
Echo answers, "Yes, you do."

CALVIN COOLIDGE

"Ah," we said; and eke "At last.
Things won't be as in the past;
Once vice-presidents were nil,
But our Fighting Calvin will
All such precedents destroy."
"Ah," we said; and "Atta boy!" . . .
Now we wonder dolefully
What's become of Calvin C.?

DR. FRANK CRANE

Daily you distribute praise
'Mong clean books and wholesome plays.
Honest toil and hard-earned gold,
Kindness to the weak and old;
Where would all the virtues be
Without such publicity?
Wealth untold you're paid, per line,
Won't you be my Valentine?

AVERY HOPWOOD

How you must have loved, when small,
Chalking words upon a wall!
"Ladies' Night" we owe to you,
"Getting Gertie's Garter," too.
Gaily gath'ring royalties
On your bedroom phantasies,
Ever heavier grows your purse
As you go from bed to worse.

FLORENZ ZIEGFELD

Still we're groggy from the blow
Dealt us—by the famous Flo;
After 1924,
He announces, nevermore
Will his shows our senses greet—
At a cost of five per seat.
Hasten, Time, your onward drive—
Welcome, 1925!

JOHN WANAMAKER

On the advertising page
Scintillates our dry good sage.
Not a text that Honest John
Cannot write a sermon on.
Readers live from day to day
Just to see what he will say.
"Have you seen his last?" they cry.
"Would to God I had," say I.

THE FAR-SIGHTED MUSE

Dark though the clouds, they are silver-lined;
  (This is the stuff that they like to read.)
If Winter comes, Spring is right behind;
  (This is the stuff that the people need.)
Smile, and the World will smile back at you;
   Aim with a grin, and you cannot miss;
Laugh off your woes, and you won't feel blue.
  (Poetry pays when it's done like this.)

Whatever it is, is completely sweet;
  (This is the stuff that will bring in gold.)
Just to be living's a perfect treat;
  (This is the stuff that will knock them cold.)
How could we, any of us, be sad?
   Always our blessings outweighing our ills;
Always there's something to make us glad.
  (This is the way you can pay your bills.)

Everything's great, in this good old world;
  (This is the stuff they can always use.)
God's in His heaven, the hill's dew-pearled;
  (This will provide for the baby's shoes.)
Hunger and War, do not mean a thing;
   Everything's rosy, where'er we roam;
Hark, how the little birds gaily sing!
  (This is what fetches the bacon home.)

PAGING SAINT PATRICK

The good Saint Patrick, in his day,
   Performed a worthy act:
He up and drove the snakes away,
   With more technique than tact.
Could he descend from realms above
   And roam about New York,
He'd find it reminiscent of
   The good old days in Cork.
The snakes he knew could never tie
   The brand our village has—
The kind that daily multiply
   And thrive on tea and jazz.

Should he his tales of snakes relate
   We'd strive to hide a laugh;
For, though the saint was wise and great,
   He didn't know the half.
Where'er he'd go, to dine or dance,
   Or lunch, or tea, or sup,
The saint would have a splendid chance
   To do some cleaning up.
Could he but leave his present star,
   He'd see that things were changed—
How sad such little visits are
   Not easily arranged!

MOOD

Unless I yield my love to you, you swear
      In strangely distant countries must you dwell;
Denied this heart of mine, you could not bear
      These dear, familiar scenes we've loved so well.
To-morrows that will come, you could not face
      With only pain to bear you company,
Among the whispering memories of this place,
      The little, intimate things that speak of me.

Where mighty mountains rear their cruel height,
      The world between us, would you dwell, apart;
Where curious peace, that comes with tropic night,
      Answers the bitter question of your heart.
The lilac bush, that bends with bloom in May,
      The winding path, the arbor where we sat.
These things should know you nevermore, you say—
      Ah, love, if I could only count on that!

TRIOLETS

Herewith I send you my heart,
        Marking it "Fragile—don't break it."
Rather a radical start—
Herewith I send you my heart;
Take it, I beg, in good part
        (That is, assuming you'll take it).
Herewith I send you my heart,
        Marking it "Fragile—don't break it."

Take me, or let me alone—
        What, after all, does it matter?
Ever my feelings you've known;
Take me, or let me alone—
Though, I might readily own,
        I'd recommend you the latter.
Take me, or let me alone—
        What, after all, does it matter?

Sweet, I have waited too long;
        Heedless and wanton I've tarried.
Silenced forever my song—
Sweet, I have waited too long.
Bitter the hemlock, and strong—
        Now you have gone and got married!
Sweet, I have waited too long;
        Heedless and wanton, I've tarried.

TO MYRTILLA, ON EASTER DAY

Myrtilla's tripping down the street,
      In Easter finery.
The Easter blooms are not more sweet
      And radiant-hued than she.
The rarest woodland violets were
      Less fragrant than her frills,
The sunny-tinted hair of her
      Would shame the daffodils.
Ah, many a heart-beat halts and skips,
      And sighs pursue her way,
As down the street Myrtilla trips,
      This joyous Easter Day.

Myrtilla's tripping gaily by,
      In Easter garb arrayed.
Ah, would the lads as deeply sigh
      For any other maid?
The lads, they come from far and near,
      When down the street she starts;
Oh, lightly step, Myrtilla dear,
      Your path is strewn with hearts.
The maids are held in envy's grips,
      For they are left, forlorn,
As down the street Myrtilla trips,
      This glorious Easter morn.

Ah, well may echo, sweet as love,
  Her laugh's delicious lilt,
For sure she knows the power of
  Her Easter bonnet's tilt;
A master wrought, with tender care,
  Each dainty frill and flounce;
The fragrance of her, cool and rare,
  Costs thirty-five per ounce.
Parisian rouge defines her lips,
  And pearls her throat bedeck—
As down the street Myrtilla trips,
  I hope she breaks her neck!

POEM IN THE AMERICAN MANNER

I dunno yer highfalutin' words, but here's th' way it seems
When I'm peekin' out th' winder o' my little House o Dreams;
I've been lookin' 'roun' this big ol' world, as bizzy as a hive,
An' I want t' tell ye, neighbor mine, it's good t' be alive.
I've ben settin' here, a-thinkin' hard, an' say, it seems t' me
That this big ol' world is jest about as good as it kin be,
With its starvin' little babies, an' its battles, an' its strikes,
An' its profiteers, an' hold-up men—th' dawggone little tykes!
An' its hungry men that fought fer us, that nobody employs.
An' I think, "Why, shucks, we're jest a lot o' grown-up little boys!"
An' I settle back, an' light my pipe, an' reach fer Mother's hand,
An' I wouldn't swap my peace o' mind fer nothin' in the land;
Fer this world uv ours, that jest was made fer folks like me an' you
Is a purty good ol' place t' live—say, neighbor, ain't it true?

FANTASY

Did we love each other, sweetest,
      Skies would be forever blue;
Time would flutter by on fleetest
      Wings of glittering golden hue.
Joy beyond a poet's telling
      Should we learn the meaning of;
Arcady would be our dwelling—
      Did we love.

Did we love each other, darling,
      Banished ugliness and gloom;
Ever sweet would pipe the starling,
      Ever gay the rose would bloom.
Care and trouble could not find us,
      Bliss untold would be our lot.
But, one scarcely need remind us,
      We do not.

MORAL TALES FOR THE YOUNG [2]

Little Gormley stole a purse.
Took it from his crippled nurse.
It was quite a lucky touch—
She'd been saving for a crutch.
So our hero, for a starter,
Bought a seat for "Gertie's Garter."
Spent in vain his gains unlawful—
For he thought the show was awful!

When *you* plunder Nursie's hoard.
Spend it where you won't be bored.

Gracie, with her golden curls,
Took her mother's string of pearls.
Figuring —as who would not?
It would pawn for quite a lot.
Picture, then, her indignation
When she found it imitation!
Though her grief she tries to smother,
Grace can't feel the same towards Mother!

All pretence and sham detest;
Work for nothing but the best.

Earnest—such a little man!
Got his family's sedan.
Drove it over hill and dale—
Just escaped the county jail—
Maimed, in his exhilaration,
Folk of spotless reputation.
But his trip with gloom was tainted—
Now the car must be repainted!

Strive to keep the death-rate low—
Think how high repair bills go!

THOUGHTS

Yes, my love, I think about you
           In the morning's roseate flush;
Heavy hang the clouds, without you,
           Sullen seems the dawning's blush.
In the slender, graceful grasses,
           Silver-tipped with sparkling dew,
In the woodland's shadowy masses
           All that I can see is you.

When the noon-day sun is burning,
           Hot the scented air, and clear,
Then to you my thoughts are turning,
           And I would that you were here.
Then I dream that, happy vagrants,
           We are wandering hand in hand
Through the lanes of light and fragrance
           Into Summer's fairyland.

When the weary sun is sinking,
           And the blossoms close, in rest,
Then of you, my love, I'm thinking,
           As I watch the brilliant west.
When the little stars show faintly
           In the Maxfield Parrish sky,
When the moon gleams, cold and saintly,
           Then to you my fancies fly.

When the frightened owls are calling,
           And the sombre midnight reigns,
Thick and fast the shades come crawling,
           Like the thoughts of fevered brains,
When life trembles at the brink of
           Death's unfathomable deep,
You're the last thing that I think of—
           Goodness knows, I need some sleep.

MEN I'M NOT MARRIED TO

No matter where my route may lie,
       No matter whither I repair,
In brief—no matter how or why
       Or when I go, the boys are there.
On lane and byway, street and square,
       On alley, path and avenue,
They seem to spring up everywhere—
       The men I am not married to.

I watch them as they pass me by;
       At each in wonderment I stare,
And "But for heaven's grace," I cry,
       "There goes the guy whose name I'd bear!"
They represent no species rare,
       They walk and talk as others do;
They're fair to see—but only fair—
       The men I am not married to.

I'm sure that to a mother's eye
       Is each potentially a bear;
But though at home they rank ace-high,
       No change of heart could I declare.
Yet worry silvers not their hair;
       They deck them not with sprigs of rue.
It's curious how they do not care—
       The men I am not married to.

     L'Envoi
In fact, if they'd a chance to share
       Their lot with me, a lifetime through,
They'd doubtless tender me the air—
       The men I am not married to.

WOODLAND SONG

The hothouses' offerings, costly and rare,
      Cannot ape the forget-me-not's blue;
Blooms forced to perfection can't hope to compare
      With the lowly anemone's hue.
The humble wild rose, unassuming and meek,
      Must have stolen the setting sun's glow;
The blushes which play o'er its delicate cheek
      Are of tints that no palette may know.

No matter how lovely these flowers may be,
Gardenias and orchids look better to me.

The purple-eyed violet, fragrantly cool,
      Spends its beauty extravagantly.
The waxen-white lily that sleeps on the pool
      Gives its loveliness lavishly free.
Their glorious petals the poppies unfold
      For whoever may happen to pass,
And Nature, made mad by the buttercups' gold,
      Flings it wantonly over the grass.

But my favorite blossoms, I'm here to aver,
Are American Beauties at five dollars per.

POLLYANNA GETS THE AIR

So many others had gone before—
       Didn't I know that I'd not be last?
So many names on his heart he wore—
       Didn't I know it would soon be past?
Ever I saw, as my day ran by,
       From the beginning, the end thereof;
Gladly and eagerly, though, did I
       Give him my love.

Gaily we sped through our golden day—
       Could there be grief, when he broke his vow?
Gaily I'd given my heart away—
       Could there be bitterness in it now?
Fragrant and fresh are my memories;
       Sorrow and yearning they rise above.
Tell him I never am sad—and please
       Give him my love.

RONDEAU [1]

It isn't fair, to me, when you're away.
In vain the clouds their brightest hues display.
      Sweet Summer dons in vain her gladdest guise—
      The vision falls but coldly on my eyes;
The sky seems draped in melancholy gray.

Though never bloomed the roses half so gay,
Though never half so radiant shone the day,
      This loveliness my stubborn heart denies;
      It isn't fair.

And do you, also, sing a minor lay?
Do you to bitter yearnings fall a prey?
      "Well, no," frank Echo honestly replies,
      "In fact, it is distinctly otherwise."
And that, my dear, is why again I say
      It isn't fair.

ROSEMARY [1]

Ah, no, I dare not lose myself in dreams
      Of that dead day we ne'er shall know again;
So pitifully brief a while it seems,
      So sharp the thought of you, as you were then.
The poignant memories of little things—
      A flower in your coat, a frock I wore;
The wistful autumns, and the troubling springs—
      I dare not let them come to me once more.

The tender gloamings, when we two would stray
      Where locusts hung their frothy blooms above;
The violets—like my eyes, you used to say;
      The rustic bridge, where first you spoke of love;
The words we whispered, while the summer breeze
      Fluttered the grasses with its scented breath;
Ah, no, I dare not summon thoughts like these;
      I'm so afraid I'd laugh myself to death.

SONG [1]

And shall we build a little nest
      In Arcady, in Arcady,
Where we can settle down and rest
      In sweet security;
A place where sunbeams cast their spell,
      And shadows play, and shadows play,
Where you and I and Love can dwell
      Forever and a day?

And shall we go there, you and I,
      In poppy time, in poppy time,
When fluffy cloudlets dot the sky
      And clustered roses climb?
And shall we watch the seasons wane,
      And come and go, and come and go,
And welcome April's golden rain,
      And hail December's snow?

And will no other ever find
      Our garden spot, our garden spot?
And shall we leave the world behind
      And count it well forgot?
There boundless peace can come to us,
      But trouble can't, but trouble can't.
And shall we live forever thus?
      You bet your life we shan't.

GRANDFATHER SAID IT

When I was but a little thing of two, or maybe three,
My granddad—on my mother's side—would lift me on his knee;
He'd take my thumb from out my mouth and say to me: "My dear,
Remember what I tell you when you're choosing a career:

"Take in laundry work; cart off dust;
Drive a moving van if you must;
Shovel off the pavement when the snow lies white;
But think of your family, and please don't write."

When I was two I cannot say his counsel knocked me cold.
But now it all returns—for, darling, I am growing old,
And when I read the writing of the authors of today
I echo all those golden words that grandpa used to say:

"Clean out ferryboats; peddle fish;
Go be chorus men if you wish;
Rob your neighbors' houses in the dark midnight;
But think of your families, and please don't write."

MONODY

Slowly the roses droop and die;
>   (Where is the love we knew of old?)
Slowly the sun-bright days go by.
>   (Little white love, so cold, so cold.)
Dark are the leaves on the weary ground,
>   Sad are the winds in the still, gray glen;
Slowly the year goes its listless round
>   Over again.

Somewhere the sunbeams dance and play;
>   (Where is the love that used to thrill?)
Somewhere the riotous roses sway.
>   (Little white love, so still, so still.)
Somewhere the skies of young April shine
>   Bright as the heavens we prayed to then . . .
Somewhere you're pulling the same old line
>   Over again.

SOMEWHAT DELAYED SPRING SONG

Crocuses are springing,
Birds are lightly winging,
Corydon is singing
      To his rustic lute;
Sullen winter passes,
Shepherds meet their lasses,
Tender-tinted grasses
      Shoot.

All the world's a-thrilling,
Meadow larks are shrilling,
Little brooks are trilling,
      You, alone, are mute;
Why do you delay it?
Love's a game——let's play it,
Go ahead and say it——
      Shoot!

SONNET [1]

Sweeter your laugh than trill of lark at dawn.
       As marble richly gleams, so shines your throat.
The grace of you would shame the pale young fawn;
       Rather than walk, like silken down you float.
Lighter your touch than fall of April rain;
       Cooler your cheek than petal washed with dew.
Whene'er you speak, all gladness and all pain
       Speak also, in the throbbing voice of you.

Like blossom on its stem is poised your head,
       Wrapped closely round about with fragrant bands.
As roses' passionate hearts, your mouth is red;
       Like lilies in the wind, your long white hands.
Brighter the glance of you than summer star;
       But, lady fair, how awful thick you are!

TO A LADY

Lady, pretty lady, delicate and sweet,
    Timorous as April, frolicsome as May,
Many are the hearts that lie beneath your feet
    As they go a-dancing down the sunlit way.

Lady, pretty lady, blithe as trilling birds,
    Shy as early sunbeams play your sudden smile.
How you quaintly prattle lilting baby words,
    Fluttering your helpless little hands the while!

Lady, pretty lady, bright your eyes and blue,
    Who could be a-counting all the hearts they broke?
Not a man you meet that doesn't fall for you;
    Lady, pretty lady, how I hope you choke!

MEMORIES

Once, you say, we felt love's blisses
    When the world was not so wise;
Once, you say, you knew my kisses
    Under Babylonian skies.
There fulfilled our scorching passion,
    There we pledged our tender vow—
Strange we meet in this cold fashion
    Here and now.

Maybe you were, as you've stated,
    Fooling round in Babylon;
Maybe you participated
    In the local goings-on.
Maybe things like that befell you,
    Ages past. But anyhow,
I was never there, I'll tell you
    Here and now.

PROMISE

Love beyond my maddest dreaming
> You have sworn you'll show to me;

You will guide me to the gleaming,
> Reeling heights of ecstasy.

Dizzier joy than else could reach me,
> Fiercer bliss and wilder thrill,

All of this some day you'll teach me,
> Y-e-e-s you will!

RONDEAU [2]

Give me a rose, cool-petaled, virgin white,
Pure as the morning, mystical as night;
   Not bold gardenias, flaunting their expense
   Like courtesans, in perfumed insolence,
Nor brazen orchids, feverishly bright.

Give me no hothouse violets, cold, polite,
With lengths of costly ribbon girdled tight—
   Matrons, in corseted magnificence;
      Give me a rose.

One girlish blossom proffer as your mite.
Ah, lovelier by far within my sight
   Than rich exotics' glamorous pretense
   Is one shy rose, sweet in its diffidence.
And then besides, my love, the price is right;
      Give me a rose.

SONG OF THE CONVENTIONS

We'd dance, with grapes in our wind-tossed hair,
      And garments of swirling smoke;
We'd fling wild song to the amorous air,
      Till the long-dead gods awoke.
Our quivering bodies, young and white,
      Poised light by the brooklet's brink,
We'd whirl and leap through the moon-mad night—
      But what would the neighbors think?

We'd bid the workaday world go hang,
      And idle the seasons through;
We'd pay no tribute of thought or pang
      To the world that once we knew.
With hearts in ecstasy intertwined,
      In languorous, sweet content,
We'd leave all worry and care behind—
      But how would we pay the rent?

We'd roam the universe, hand in hand,
      Through tropical climes, or cold,
And find each spot was a wonderland,
      A country of pearl and gold.
Our hearts as light as the sunlit foam,
      We'd voyage the oceans o'er,
With never a thought for those at home—
      But wouldn't our folks be sore?

SONG [2]

Clarabelle has golden hair,
      Mabel's eyes are blue,
Nancy's form is passing fair,
      Mary's heart is true.
Chloë's heart has proved to be
      Something else again;
Not so much on looks is she
      But she gets the men.

Doris deals in verse and prose,
      Stella's brow is high,
Martha, swift and skillful, sews,
      Maud can bake a pie.
Chloë neither sews nor cooks,
      Cannot swing a pen,
Doesn't seem to run to books;
      She just gets the men.

Winnie's gayly dancing feet
      Fly on fairy wings;
Silver bells ring, clear and sweet,
      When Belinda sings.
Fair and true and talented
      Are they all—but then
Little Chloë knocks them dead;
      Chloë gets the men.

BALLADE OF UNDERSTANDABLE AMBITIONS

Fame and honor and high degree,
  Jeweled scepter and throne-room plot—
Yellow primroses, they, to me;
  Milder longings are mine, God wot.
Smooth and simple, I'd have my lot;
  I'd depart on another tack.
At my aim give me just one shot—
  All I want is a lot of jack.

Fond communion with field and tree,
  Bread and cheese in an ivied cot;
Sweet and clean though the thought may be,
  I subscribe to it ne'er a jot.
Other yearnings my heart make hot,
  Other cravings my spirit rack.
In my dreams to my goal I trot—
  All I want is a lot of jack.

On the pages of history
  Ne'er my name shall I sign and blot;
I'll go down to posterity
  Neither scholar nor patriot.
Cloaks of Shelley and Keats and Scott
  Ne'er will fall on my humble back;
Immortality ask I not—
  All I want is a lot of jack.

  L'Envoi
Prince, or Rover, or Rex, or Spot,
  Ere I die let me take a crack
At the wish which I've never got—
  All I want is a lot of jack.

"HOW BOLD IT IS"

How bold it is, this fine young love we bear;
A high, white flame, to cut the ghostly night;
A virgin armor, burnished hard and bright
To turn the blows of age and death and care!
Too brave a thing it is, to see it break
Beneath the unending taps of little things—
Of sharpened words, and hurried answerings,
And fretful illness, and recited ache,
And tiny jealousies, and whimpering woe,
And household plannings, year on futile year,
And patient "Yes, my love," and "Yes, my dear,"
And "Why did you do thus, and why do so?"

Quick, let us part, that ever our love may be
As now we know it, young and bold and free.

SONG OF A CONTENTED HEART

All sullen blares the wintry blast;
    Beneath gray waves the waters sleep.
Thick are the dizzying flakes and fast;
    The edged air cuts cruel deep.
The stricken trees gaunt limbs extend
    Like whining beggars, shrill with woe;
The cynic heavens do but send,
    In bitter answer, darts of snow.
Stark lies the earth, in misery,
    Beneath grim winter's dreaded spell—
But I have you, and you have me,
    So what the hell, love, what the hell!

The wolf, he crouches at the sill,
    And, grinning, bares expectant fangs,
While heavy o'er the house, and chill,
    The coming of the landlord hangs.
Each moment, on the shrinking door,
    May sound his knocking's hideous din.
And more and more, and ever more,
    The eager bills come trooping in.
The milkman clamors for his due,
    The grocer and the cook, as well—
But you have me, and I have you,
    So what the hell, love, what the hell!

SONG OF THE WILDERNESS

We'll go out to the open spaces,
      Break the web of the morning mist,
Feel the wind on our upflung faces.
      [This, of course, is if you insist.]
We'll go out in the golden season,
      Brave-eyed, gaze at the sun o'erhead.
[Can't you listen, my love, to reason?
      Don't you know that my nose gets red?]
Where the water falls, always louder,
      Deep we'll dive, in the chuckling foam.
[I'll go big without rouge and powder!
      Why on earth don't you leave me home?]

We'll go out where the winds are playing,
      Roam the ways of the brilliant West.
[I was never designed for straying;
      In a taxi I'm at my best.]
Minds blown clean of the thoughts that rankle,
      Far we'll stray where the grasses swirl.
[I'll be certain to turn my ankle;
      Can't you dig up another girl?]
We'll go out where the light comes falling—
      Bars of amber and rose and green.
[Go, my love, if the West is calling!
      Leave me home with a magazine!]

TRIOLET [1]

Give back the heart that I gave;
      Keeping it never can mend it.
See, I can smile, and be brave.
Give back the heart that I gave,
Hold it no more as your slave—
      I've got a new place to send it.
Give back the heart that I gave;
      Keeping it never can mend it.

WANDERLUST

I want to go out to the woodlands green,
      And stand 'neath the mighty trees.
I'm longing to hark to the mournful keen—
      The voice of the wistful breeze.
I'll find me the place where the fox-gloves start,
      And violets coyly bloom,
Where the whispering cypress stands apart
      In mystical, fragrant gloom.
I'll go where the feathery grasses lean
      To gaze in the placid brook;
I want to go out to the woodlands green,
      And never give them a look.

I want to go down to the open sea;
      I'll search for a sunlit strand
Where clean-scented winds blow cool and free
      O'er glittering, swirling sand.
I want to go out on the sparkling shore
      Where frolicsome wavelets play;
I'm yearning to feel on my cheek, once more,
      The kiss of the ardent spray.
There's longing, down deep in the heart of me,
      To look on the sun-shot foam.
I want to go down to the open sea—
      And then I'll come right back home.

I want to go back to a country town,
        Afar from the city's thrills—
A dear little village that's snuggled down
        Asleep, by the guardian hills.
I'm going to stand in the ancient square
        And look to the crimson west
When pealing of chimes, on the quiet air,
        Bids villagers go to rest.
I'm yearning to dress in a gingham gown
        And play with a frisking calf.
I want to go back to a country town,
        And give it a hearty laugh.

A TRIOLET

You'll be returning, one day.
>   (Such premonitions are true ones.)
Treading the dew-spangled way,
You'll be returning, one day.
I'll have a few things to say—
>   I've learned a whole lot of new ones.
You'll be returning, one day.
>   (Such premonitions are true ones.)

PÆAN

The sun shines fair, the sun shines true,
      The sun shines golden bright;
The sky takes on a lovelier blue,
      The clouds a daintier white.
The birds trill out a roundelay,
      The rosebuds dance with glee,
Each living thing holds holiday;
      The world belongs to me!

My heart beats loud, my heart beats strong,
      My heart beats fast and high;
Within my soul's a rousing song,
      A light within my eye.
Go, raise the banners high in air,
      And spread the tidings round!
Let drums and trumpets boom and blare,
      For I have lost a pound!

SONG [3]

When summer used to linger,
      Before the daisies died,
You'd but to bend your finger
      And I was by your side.
And, oh, my heart was breaking,
      And, oh, my life was through;
You had me for the taking;
      "Now run along," said you.

But now the summer's over,
      The birds have flown away,
And all the amorous clover
      Has turned to sober hay.
And you're the one to tarry,
      And you're the one to sigh,
And beg me, will I marry.
      "The deuce I will," say I.

AND OBLIGE

When I've made a million dollars—it may take a year or two
    At the present rate of speed that things are going—
There are various little matters that are somewhat overdue,
    And the prospect, at the moment, isn't glowing;
But as soon as I've a million, as I started in to say,
    Life will be, I take it, gloriously happy;
For already I am planning to expend it in a way
    That will be, if I may say it, rather snappy.

I will charter me a taxicab of cheery white and brown,
    And you'll never catch me glancing at the meter!
And I'll make a little tour of all the milliners in town;
    And the question is, Could anything be sweeter?
Just for stamps and lunch and cigarettes, each morn I'll draw a check
    For a thousand dollars, payable to bearer,
And you'll hear the pearls a-clanking, as I drape them on my neck.
    It occurs to me that little could be fairer.

It is true that a million doesn't take you very far,
    And it's hard to find another when you've shot it;
But I'll blow it like the widely known inebriated tar,
    For I want to be a good one while I've got it.
So the minute I've a million, I'll go right ahead and spend,
    Though it doesn't last me more than over Sunday.
In the meantime, though, I wonder, as a favor to a friend,
    Could you let me have a dollar—say, till Monday?

TRIOLET [2]

It is never the cost of the gift;
        It is the thought that I treasure.
Such affections as mine do not shift.
It is never the cost of the gift—
Which is quite an incentive to thrift;
        Business must come before pleasure.
It is never the cost of the gift;
        It is the thought that I treasure.

BALLADE OF A NOT INSUPPORTABLE LOSS

Who will slacken the mental strain,
     Who'll sit down and explain to me.
This, the riddle that racks my brain,
     This, the theme of my monody?
     I'm a glutton for mystery—
Plots and puzzles to me are clear;
     Just one thing has me up a tree—
Where did the flappers disappear?

What's become of that mighty train.
     All so carefully bold and free.
Each like each, as were drops of rain.
     Short of garment, and frank of knee?
     Do they flap in eternity?
All I know is, they are not here;
     To the riddle, I hold no key—
Where did the flappers disappear?

Think not, reader, that I'd complain.
     Squander on me no sympathy.
Though they've vanished, I feel no pain—
     I get on—rather swimmingly.
     I'd not cavil at Fate's decree;
Rather, give it a rousing cheer,
     Still, there's something I cannot see—
Where did the flappers disappear?

     L'Envoi
Prince, you've labored incredibly
     Tracing the snows of yesteryear;
Answer this one, and let that be—
     Where did the flappers disappear?

SONG OF A HOPEFUL HEART

Oh, time of our lyrical laughter,
   Oh, pageant of glittering days,
The glamourous Aprils—and after,
   The delicate, mystical Mays!
So gallant and sudden and heedless,
   So gayly defiant of regret,
We smiled as we thought how 'twas needless
   To vow that we'd never forget
Those galloping days of our blisses,
   Alike, and yet never the same—
But you have forgotten my kisses,
   And I have forgotten your name.

Oh, always there's one who remembers,
   Who brightens, with memories' glow,
The ponderous, sullen Novembers,
   The colorless Winters, and slow.
Why linger in shadowy sadness?
   Why drape us in lavender hue?
The red of that magical madness
   Our hearts could be wearing anew.
It's only the coward who misses
   The glorious rush of the game—
Try hard to remember my kisses;
   I guess I can think of your name.

SONG [4]

When all the world was younger.
       When petals lay as snow.
What recked I of the hunger
       An empty heart can know?
For love was young and cheery,
       And love was quick and free;
To-morrow might be weary,
       But when was that to me?

But now the world is older,
       And now to-morrow's come.
The winds are rushing colder,
       And all the birds are dumb.
And icy shackles fetter
       The brooklet's sunny blue—
And I was never better;
       But what is that to you?

SONG FOR AN APRIL DUSK

Tell me tales of a lilied pool
        Asleep beneath the sun.
Tell me of woodlands deep and cool,
        When chuckling satyrs run.
Tell me, in light and tinkling words,
        Of rippling, lilting streams.
Tell me of radiant-breasted birds,
        Who sing their amorous dreams.
Tell of the doomed butterfly
        That flings his hour away.
Fated to live and love and die
        Before the death of day.

Tell me tales of the moon-pale sprites
        Whose beauty none may know.
Tell me of secret, silver nights
        When great red stars are low.
Tell of the virgin Spring, the fair,
        Who roams the circling years.
Rain-drops strung in her fragrant hair,
        Her eyes a-mist with tears.
Tell me of elves, who leap to kiss,
        Who trip the velvet sward.
Tell me stories of things like this,
        And, boy, will I be bored!

ROSEMARY [2]

I wear your fragrant memory, like a spray of mignonette,
      As I tread the winding ribbon of the years.
How clear the radiant image of you stands before me yet
      In the thousand little mirrors of my tears.
And ah, my dearest love, when I forget the way to dream
      I'll forget your silent nearness in the dark,
Where languorous lilies floated on a quiet woodland stream—
      Or were you the one I'd meet in Central Park?
The love of you was sudden and the heart of you was strong;
      There were leaping little devils in your eyes;
Your laughter rode the morning like a joyous May-day song—
      No, I guess that must have been two other guys.

Could I forget your April smile, the shining way of you,
      Could I forget your method so adroit?
Could I forget those stories of the other girls you knew?
      Or was that the butter-and-egg man from Detroit?
A pair of truant children, we would often steal away
      Where the city's voice was gloriously mute,
And plan the little cottage we should have, one happy day—
      Or were you the boy that had the wife in Butte?
You had my first, my golden love, and though we're torn apart,
      Through all the circling years, I've been the same.
Your name is ever written on the pages of my heart—
      And, by the way, my dear, what *was* your name?

BALLADE OF A COMPLETE FLOP

Sad the matter of which I speak,
      Deep the trouble of which I sigh.
To the heavens my woes I shriek—
      I'd just love to sit down and cry.
      Though I hate to admit it, my
Batting av'rage is less than fair.
      Generous gentlemen pass me by—
All that they give me is the air.

Rich man, beggarman, merchant, sheik,
      Actor, congressman, human fly.
Argentinean, Czech, and Greek
      Give and give, till the well runs dry,
      Gifts of elderly Scotch and rye.
Gifts of jewels and orchids rare
      To a more competent Lorelei—
All that they give me is the air.

What's the matter with my technique?
      I can't fathom, or even try.
I'm intelligent, fond, and weak—
      Why don't I get a regular guy?
      Just for others, the goose hangs high;
All love's tokens that form my share
      May be placed in a pig's left eye—
All that they give me is the air.

    L'Envoi
Princes, tell me the reason why.
      What's the trouble, and how, and where?
When did Santa Claus go and die?
      All that they give me is the air.

FOLK SONG

Robin, he is strong and sure,
        Gallant, wise, and gay.
Gavin's heart is calm and pure
        As the new-born day.
Steady shine young Alan's eyes,
        Deep with honesty.
Jack, he tells me naught but lies—
        He's the lad for me.

Richard vows no other maid
        Did he love before.
Will, his beating heart he laid
        At my cottage door.
Peter tells me, "None but you
        Am I thinking of."
Jack, he's wondrously untrue—
        He's my own dear love.

Casper's hair is golden brown;
        Hal is straight and slim.
Martin's richest in the town—
        Who'd say "no" to him?
Rafe's a fine young gentleman;
        Tom's with virtue blest.
Jack, he broke my heart and ran—
        I love him the best.

BALTO

(The Lead Dog of the Team That Brought Antitoxin to Nome)

I think that you could only pity me
       Who'd want to weep and stroke your head and coo
And murmur little names, mellifluously,
       And know no other thing to do.

What should I do, but drop my eyes, and strain
       To cloak the meanness of my offerings,
Who am aggrieved at cold, and hide from pain,
       And live with little, little things.

My days slip by in thin and wavering line;
       Softened my life to such as sick men lead.
And sharp there cuts across dimmed hours like mine
       The cold white radiance of your deed.

Outraging cornered Death, you held the course
       Against the whining night, the whirling day.
When man gave over to the inhuman force,
       Then it was you who led the way.

Though never trumpet urged you to the fight,
       And roystering rush of war was not your part,
Your spirit was a rocket in the night,
       You bore a banner in your heart.

Not hope of cited glory led you then,
       Simply, so went your days since they began.
You did the thing, nor thought of it again,
       A very gallant gentleman.

CASSANDRA DROPS INTO VERSE

We'd break the city's unfeeling clutch
        And back to good Mother Earth we'd go,
With birds and blossoms and such-and-such,
        And love and kisses and so-and-so.
We'd build a bungalow, white and green,
        With rows of hollyhocks, all sedate.
And you'd come out on the five-eighteen
        And meet me down at the garden gate.

We'd leave the city completely flat
        And dwell with chickens and cows and bees,
'Mid brooks and bowers and this and that,
        And joys and blisses and those and these.
We'd greet together the golden days,
        And hail the sun in the morning sky.
We'd find an Eden—to coin a phrase—
        The sole inhabitants, you and I.

With sweet simplicity all our aim,
        We'd fare together to start anew
In peace and quiet and what's-its-name,
        And soul communion, or what have you?
But oh, my love, if we made the flight,
        I see the end of our pastoral plan. . . .
Why, you'd be staying in town each night,
        And I'd elope with the furnace man.

MEETING-PLACE

Here the sky is clear and deep—
      Tedious heart, be gay, be gay!
One and one, like counted sheep,
      Clouds go gamboling away.
(Mary, robed in white and blue,
      Let him swear he has been true.)

Here the leaves are cool and slow—
      Then be quiet, shrieking mind!
And the gracious boughs are low,
      And the roots are sure and kind.
(Lord, that died upon a tree,
      Let him lie, and comfort me.)

SONG OF AMERICANS RESIDENT IN FRANCE

Oh, we are the bold expatriate band!
Allegiance we vow to our chosen land.
How gladly we'd offer our all to France.
We'd give her our honor, our souls, our pants.
We hail her the highest of earthly heavens;
We wriggle our shoulders, and cross our 7's.
With tolerant laughter we rock and sway
Whenever we think of the U.S.A.
At Yankee behavior we writhe and blench.
Our English is rusty—we think in French.
The Sorrows of France disarrange our sleep;
With Gallic abandon we bleed, we weep.
We long to lay down for her all we have;
We love her, we love her, *la belle, la brave!*
We'd see given back to her all her due—
The grandeur, the glory that once she knew.
We'd have her triumphantly hung with flowers,
Acknowledged supremest of all the Powers,
Her dominance written in white and black . . .
But, boy, we'd be sore if the franc came back!

RHYME OF AN INVOLUNTARY VIOLET

When I ponder lovely ladies
Slipping sweetly down to Hades,
Hung and draped with glittering booty—
Am I distant, cold and snooty?
Though I know the price their pearls are
Am I holier than the girls are?
Though they're lavish with their "Yes's,"
Do I point, and shake my tresses?
No! I'm filled with awe and wonder.
I review my every blunder . . .
Do I have the skill to tease a
Guy for an Hispano-Suiza?
I can't even get me taxis
Off to Sydneys, Abes, and Maxies!
Do the pretty things I utter
To the kings of eggs and butter
Gain me pearls as big as boulders,
Clattering, clanking round my shoulders,
Advertising, thus, their full worth?
No, my dear. Mine come from Woolworth.
Does my smile across a table
Win a cloak of Russian sable?
Baby, no. I'd have to kill a
Man to get a near-chinchilla.
Men that come on for conventions
Show me brotherly intentions;
Though my glance be fond and melting,
Do they ever start unbelting
With the gifts they give the others?

No! They tell me of their mothers,
To the baby's pictures treat me,
Say they want the wife to meet me!
Gladly I'd be led to slaughter
Where the ermine flows like water,
When the gay white globes are lighted;
But I've never been invited!
So my summary, in fact, is
What an awful flop my act is!

THE TEMPTRESS

You'd think, with all the age and sense
It has by now, that Providence
Would overlook my vaporings,
And turn its mind to bigger things.
You'd think, compared with flood and war,
My small concerns would be a bore.
But no! The world may go to pot
While I have service no one got.
For do I stretch myself, and smile,
And bask in peace a little while,
And rashly murmur, "Here is bliss"—
It cries, "We must look into this!
Too full her cup to bear a drop;
Well, well, this thing has got to stop."
Or do I weep me harsh and dry,
And raise my futile fists on high,
And curse my dam, and sob, and sweat—
It says, "She ain't seen nothing yet"
(Considering this the latest slang).
So letting all the world go hang,
It sets itself to showing me
What true unhappiness may be.
Ah, could I tempt assorted gents
As sure as I can Providence,
A different story I'd rehearse,
And damned if I'd be writing verse!

TO ELSPETH

Lady, I have read your verse on
Me—the one wherein you write
"How I'd like to meet that person
All alone some ebon night!"

Though your wish to wound were little,
You have done your worst—you see,
Some one, when my heart was brittle,
Said those very words to me.

Lady, take my humble greetings;
Take my thanks; but let me say
Were it not for midnight meetings,
I'd be on my feet to-day.

WHEN WE WERE VERY SORE

(Lines on Discovering That You Have Been Advertised as
America's A. A. Milne.)

Dotty had
Great Big
Visions of
Quietude.
Dotty saw an
Ad, and it
Left her
Flat.
Dotty had a
Great Big
Snifter of
Cyanide.
And that (said Dotty)
Is that.

THE ACCURSED

Oh, I shall be, till Gabriel's trump,
Nostalgic for some distant dump;
And ever doomed to weep me dry
For some lost mediocre guy.

CHRIS-CROSS

On Confusing Messrs. Morley and Robin

Christopher Morley goes hippetty, hoppetty,
Hippetty, hippetty, hop.
Whenever I ask him politely to stop it, he
Says he can't possibly stop. . . .

GRANDE PASSION

If you should break your beauteous nose,
My love would perish, I suppose;
Or did your hair go limp and straight,
I might again be celibate.
Were you to slide your step, and peer,
You'd see my little back, I fear;
But lose, my love, your soul and sense—
I should not know the difference.

EXCURSION INTO ASSONANCE

I have trodden level sand
        Along a reach of gray—
From dune-top to sea's end,
        No breathing thing but me.

I have dropped the heavy latch
        Against the rain's tap,
And shivered by the fire, to watch
        The dark hours slip.

The desolate beach, the midnight storm—
        I dwelt alone with these;
But here, within your bended arm,
        Is loneliness.

—AND RETURN

I walked upon a vacant shore
      Beneath a low and thickening sky;
I faced the empty sea, and swore,
      "There is no lonelier one than I."

I waited through a night of lead;
      I heard the showers slide and hiss,
And started at my voice, that said,
      "No loneliness has been but this."

But here, my heart against your own,
      Your petulant kiss to silence me,
I know that I had never known
      How bitter lonely I could be.

SONG OF SOCIAL LIFE IN HOLLYWOOD

One speculates—or doesn't one?
Upon our movie actors' fun;
For it is true as it is right
They don't make pictures all the night.
Now what can there be left, to please
Such fortunates, in hours of ease?
Who labors for his daily bread
Rehearsing scenes would knock you dead
'Mid groves designed, as if by fairies,
For love, and its subsidiaries,
And every lithe and gifted hero
Makes whoopee, *à la mode de* Nero,
With women, wine, and even song,
The livelong day, the live day long—
What's his for fun, when work is through?
What can he do, what DOES he do?
Oh, ask me that, for I have found
There is a rule the world around;
The busman, in his hours of play,
Doth ride a bus, for holiday.

SONNET [2]

In seemly burial, love may not rest;
      A newer love must come to bear away
      The unwanted body of the dead, and lay
The wraith that stalks the heart, a tedious guest.
Let them that knew no fullness go protest
      Their vacant hearts; thus boldly may they say
      That know not haunted night and troubled day.
None who has loved bears now an empty breast.

Weary and waiting, ever on and on,
      Cold love, uncoffined, walks its rut of woe;
Only the live can bid the dead begone—
      The new must come, before the old may go.
And they alone may end the mournful tale
And cry "Farewell!" who first have uttered "Hail!"

LETTER TO OGDEN NASH

Chalet La Bruyere, Montana-Vermala, Switzerland

Dear Sir, I trust you will pardon this intrusion of an Old Subscriber
Who used to dabble for a living in rhyme, as well as vers libre,
But has now Got Away From It All, owing to a plethora of
   intellectuals,
Racquet Club members, players on two pianos, raconteurs, and
   homosectuals.
I want very much to tell you that were you on an Alp, as I'm,
You would get Ogden Nash's verses though you had to commit
   arson or m'hy'm.
I little thought, at my time of life, to be anxiously awaiting the
   New Yorker,
(Although I do not buy it, but borrow my friends', thus contributing
   nothing to the stockholders' exchorquer)
But now it's my whitest hope, for I think you are considerably
   greater
Than Walter Savage Landor, Walter de la Mare, Walter
   Winchell, and Walter Pater,
I wish you all successes, in life as in lit'rature,
And I remain your respectful admirer from the very bottom of
   my coeur.

AFTER DAWN

Theodore Dreiser
Should ought to write nicer.

SONG IN THE WORST POSSIBLE TASTE

For a Certain Mr. S., Who Got Personal

I shall not see—and don't I know 'em?
A critic lovely as a poem.

OUR COUSINS

Ever I view those people dumbly
Surnamed Mainwaring or Cholmondeley;
Folk at home my sapience staggers
Schooled at Magdalen or Jesus.
Never have I ascertained
Why they all are so refined—
Why aloofness sheds its spell
On the littlest boy or girl—
Why they're stiffer than a bible
On a solid oaken table.
Though I puzzle, make no head I can—
That's for being un-American.

BLURB

An instrument that is far from rifty
Is *The Melancholy Lute* ($2.50).

THE PASSIONATE SCREEN WRITER TO HIS LOVE

Oh come, my love, and join with me
The oldest infant industry.
Come seek the bourne of palm and pearl,
The lovely land of Boy-Meets-Girl.
Come grace this lotus-laden shore,
This Isle of Do-What's-Done-Before.
Come, curb the new, and watch the old win,
Out where the streets are paved with Goldwyn.
Here let me guide your sedulous pen
To trace the proven lines again;
Here ply your quill, in glory dipt,
And see what happens to your script;
Hear how your phrases—metered, guarded—
With actors' jokes are interlarded.
Oh, come, my love, nor fret the while
The mighty disregard your smile,
For Cohens, in this haughty small burg,
Bow but to God [Who's cut by Thalberg].
Oh, cast your scruples to the winds
And join us Pegasus' behinds!
Come, learn along with me, my sweet,
How charming thrice a day to eat,
How good to bend the stubborn neck
And hail the rhythmic weekly cheque!
But when, my love, you have been here
A little less than half a year,
You start to talk, who once were dumb,
Of "what a wondrous medium,"
And "why, they haven't scratched the surface,"
[While grieved Mnemosyne hides her face]
And "here the writer's noblest art"—
That day, my perjured love, we part!

THREAT TO A FICKLE LADY

Sweet Lady Sleep, befriend me;
    In pretty mercy, hark.
Your charming manners, tend me—
    Let down your lovely dark.

Sweet lady, take me to you,
    Becalm mine eyes, my breath. . . .
Remember, I that woo you
    Have but to smile at Death. . . .

PECKING ORDER (OR "EGGS TEMPORE")

Higgledy Piggledy, my white hen;
She lays eggs for gentlemen.
You cannot persuade her with gun or lariat
To come across for the proletariat.

The
"Hate Verses"

WOMEN

A Hate Song

I hate Women;
They get on my nerves.

There are the Domestic ones.
They are the worst.
Every moment is packed with Happiness.
They breathe deeply
And walk with large strides, eternally hurrying home
To see about dinner.
They are the kind
Who say, with a tender smile, "Money's not everything."
They are always confronting me with dresses,
Saying, "I made this myself."
They read Woman's pages and try out the recipes.
Oh, how I hate that kind of woman.

Then there are the human Sensitive Plants;
The Bundles of Nerves.
They are different from everybody else; they even tell you so.
Someone is always stepping on their feelings.
Everything hurts them—deeply.
Their eyes are forever filling with tears.
They always want to talk to me about the Real Things,
The things that Matter.
Yes, they know they could write.
Conventions stifle them.
They are always longing to get away—Away from It All!
—I wish to Heaven they would.

And then there are those who are always in Trouble.
Always.
Usually they have Husband-trouble.
They are Wronged.
They are the women whom nobody—understands.

They wear faint, wistful smiles.
And, when spoken to, they start.
They begin by saying they must suffer in silence.
No one will ever know—
And then they go into details.

Then there are the Well-Informed ones.
They are pests.
They know everything on earth
And will tell you about it gladly.
They feel it their mission to correct wrong impressions
They know Dates and Middle names.
They absolutely ooze Current Events.
Oh, how they bore me.

There are the ones who simply cannot Fathom
Why all the men are mad about them.
They say they've tried and tried.
They tell you about someone's husband;
What he said
And how he looked when he said it.
And then they sigh and ask,
"My dear, what is there about me?"
—Don't you hate them?

There are the unfailingly Cheerful ones.
They are usually unmarried.
They are always busy making little Gifts
And planning little surprises.
They tell me to be, like them, always looking on the Bright Side.
They ask me what they would do without their sense of humor?
I sometimes yearn to kill them.
Any jury would acquit me.

I hate Women;
They get on my nerves.

MEN

A Hate Song

I hate Men;
They irritate me.

I

There are the Serious Thinkers—
There ought to be a law against them.
They see life, as through shell-rimmed glasses, darkly.
They are always drawing their weary hands
Across their wan brows.
They talk about Humanity
As if they had just invented it;
They have to keep helping it along.
They revel in strikes
And they are eternally getting up petitions.
They are doing a wonderful thing for the Great Unwashed—
They are living right down among them.
They can hardly wait
For "The Masses" to appear on the newsstands,
And they read all those Russian novels—
The sex best sellers.

II

There are the Cave Men—
The Specimens of Red-Blooded Manhood.
They eat everything very rare,
They are scarcely ever out of their cold baths,
And they want everybody to feel their muscles.
They talk in loud voices,
Using short Anglo-Saxon words.
They go around raising windows,

And they slap people on the back,
And tell them what they need is exercise.
They are always just on the point of walking to San Francisco,
Or crossing the ocean in a sailboat,
Or going through Russia on a sled—
I wish to God they would!

III

And then there are the Sensitive Souls
Who do interior decorating, for Art's sake.
They always smell faintly of vanilla
And put drops of sandalwood on their cigarettes.
They are continually getting up costume balls
So that they can go
As something out of the "Arabian Nights."
They give studio teas
Where people sit around on cushions
And wish they hadn't come.
They look at a woman languorously, through half-closed eyes,
And tell her, in low, passionate tones,
What she ought to wear.
Color is everything to them—everything;
The wrong shade of purple
Gives them a nervous breakdown.

IV

Then there are the ones
Who are Simply Steeped in Crime.
They tell you how they haven't been to bed
For four nights.
They frequent those dramas
Where the only good lines
Are those of the chorus.
They stagger from one cabaret to another,
And they give you the exact figures of their gambling debts.
They hint darkly at the terrible part

That alcohol plays in their lives.
And then they shake their heads
And say Heaven must decide what is going to become of them—
I wish I were Heaven!

I hate Men;
They irritate me.

ACTRESSES
A Hate Song

I hate Actresses;
They get on my nerves.

There are the Adventuresses,
The Ladies with Lavender Pasts.
They wear gowns that show all their emotions,
And they simply can't stop undulating.
The only stage properties they require
Are a box of cigarettes and a package of compromising letters.
Their Big Scene invariably takes place in the hero's apartment.
They are always hanging around behind screens
And overhearing things about the heroine.
They go around clutching their temples
And saying, Would to God they were good—
Would to God they were!

There are the Wronged Ones;
The Girls Whose Mothers Never Told Them.
In the first act they wear pink gingham sunbonnets
And believe implicitly in the stork.
In the third act they are clad in somber black
And know that there isn't any Santa Claus.
They are always going out into the night.
They faint a great deal,
And if anyone lets them get near the center of the stage
They immediately burst into hysterics.
They unfortunately never commit suicide until the last act—
It's always the audience that pays and pays and pays.

Then there are the Musical Comedy Stars;
The press-agent's livelihood.
They sing about love—in waltz time—
And they dance as if something were just about to break.
They end by appearing in a piece of court plaster

And an American flag,
And then the audience has to stand up.
The show isn't considered a success
Until they climb into a flower-wreathed swing,
And swing far out, over the orchestra—
Oh, that I might be there when the ropes break.

And there are the Emotional Ones;
The ones who say,
"I'll have two lumps of sugar in my tea, please,"
In exactly the same tones as they say
"Yes, it was I who murdered him."
They are forever tearing their hair—
I hope it hurts them.
They shriek at everything,
Usually at the hero,
And they hurl themselves on the floor at his feet
And say that they wish it were all over—
They said something.

Then there are the child Actresses
Who should be unseen and not heard.
They go around telling people about Heaven
As if they were special correspondents.
They are always climbing up on innocent bystanders
And asking them why they look so sad;
They eternally bring their fathers and mothers together,
Which is always an error of judgment.
They never fail to appear in their nightgowns
And then kneel down beside the orchestra leader,
And say their prayers to the spotlight man—
I wish I were Commodore Gerry.

I hate Actresses;
They get on my nerves.

RELATIVES
A Hate Song

I hate Relatives;
They cramp my style.

There are Aunts.
Even the best of us have them.
They are always dropping in for little visits,
And when you ask them to stay,
They take it seriously.
They never fail to tell you how badly you look;
And they relate little anecdotes
About friends of theirs who went into Declines.
Their conversation consists entirely of Insides;
They are never out of a Critical Condition.
They are always posing for X-ray portraits
Of parts of their anatomy with names like parlor-cars.
They say the doctor tells them
That they have only one chance in a hundred—
The odds aren't big enough.

Then there are In-Laws,
The Necessary Evils of Matrimony.
The only things they don't say about you
Are the ones they can't pronounce.
No matter what you do,
They know a better way to do it.
They are eternally searching your house for dust;
If they can't find any,
It is a wasted day.
They are always getting their feelings hurt
So that they can go around with martyred expressions
And say that you will appreciate them when they're gone—
You certainly will.

There are Nephews;
They are the lowest form of animal life.
They are forever saying bright things
And there is no known force that can keep them
From reciting little pieces about Our Flag.
They have the real Keystone sense of humor—
They are always firing things off in your ear,
Or pulling away the chair you are about to sit on.
Whenever you are striving to impress anyone,
They always appear
And try out the new words they learned from the ice-man—
I wish the Government would draft all males under ten!

And then there are Husbands;
The White Woman's Burden.
They never notice when you wear anything new—
You have to point it out.
They tell you about the deal they put through,
Or the approach they made,
And you are supposed to get all worked up.
They are always hanging around outside your door
And they are incessantly pulling out watches,
And saying, "Aren't you dressed yet?"
They were never known to be wrong;
Everything is always your fault.
And whenever you go out to have a good time,
You always meet them—
I wish to Heaven somebody would alienate their affections.

I hate Relatives;
They cramp my style.

SLACKERS
A Hate Song

I hate Slackers;
They get on my nerves.

There are the Conscientious Objectors.
They are the real German atrocities.
They go around saying, "War is a terrible thing,"
As if it were an original line.
They take the war as a personal affront;
They didn't start it—and that lets them out.
They point out how much harder it is
To stay at home and take care of their consciences
Than to go and have some good, clean fun in a nice, comfortable
  trench.
They explain that it isn't a matter of mere bravery;
They only wish they had the chance to suffer for their convictions—
I hope to God they get their wish!

Then there are the Socialists;
The Professional Bad Sports.
They don't want anybody to have any fun.
If anybody else has more than two dollars,
They consider it a criminal offense.
They look as if the chambermaid forgot to dust them.
There is something about their political views
That makes them wear soiled decolleté shirts,
And they are too full of the spirit of brotherhood
To ask any fellow creature to cut their hair.
They are always telling their troubles to the New Republic;
And are forever blocking the traffic with parades.
If anyone disagrees with them
They immediately go on strike.
They will prove—with a street corner and a soap box—
That the whole darned war was Morgan's fault—
Boy, page an alienist.

There are the Pacifists;
They have chronic stiff necks
From turning the other cheek,
They say they don't believe in war—
As if it were Santa Claus or the Stork.
They will do anything on earth to have peace
Except go out and win it.
Of course they are the only people
Who disapprove of war;
Everybody else thinks it's perfectly great—
The Allies are only fighting
Because it keeps them out in the open air
They know that if we'd all go around wearing lilies,
And simply refusing to fight,
The Kaiser would take his army and go right back home.
It's all wrong, Pershing, it's all wrong.

And then there are the Men of Affairs;
The ones who are too busy to fight.
Business is too good,
And men aren't needed yet, anyway—
Wait till the Germans come over here.
They tell you it would be just their luck
To waste three or four months in a training camp,
And then have peace declared.
It isn't as if they hadn't dependents;
Their wives' relatives can barely buy tires for the Rolls-Royce.
Of course, they may be called in the draft,
But they know they can easily get themselves exempted,
Because they have every symptom of hay fever—
I wish I were head of the draft board!

I hate Slackers;
They get on my nerves.

BOHEMIANS

A Hate Song

I hate Bohemians;
They shatter my morale.

There are the Artists;
The Inventors of the Nude,
They are always gesticulating with their thumbs,
And sketching, with forks, on table cloths;
They point out all the different colors in a sunset
As if they were trying to sell it to you;
They are forever messing around with batik;
And hanging yellow tassels on things;
And stencilling everything within reach.
I do hope that Gibson never learns what they think of him:
It would simply break his heart.
Of course, they know that being hung in the Academy
Is just a matter of pull.
They say that James Montgomery Flagg may stoop to mere success,
But as for them,
Let them starve first!
Fair enough!

There are the Writers;
The Press Agents for Sex.
They are forever exposing their inmost souls,
Their "stuff" is always "brutally frank"—
Why, they'd just as soon tell you their favorite flower.
They find their fullest expression in free verse;
They call it that
Because they have to give it away.
They are extremely well read,
They can quote from their own works for hours—
Without a mistake.
They are always pulling manuscripts out of their pockets,
And asking you to tell them, honestly—is it too daring?

They would sit down
And write the Great American Novel
If they only could find a publisher Big Enough.
Oh, well—
Genius is an infinite capacity for giving pains.

There are the Actors;
They always refer to themselves as "Players."
Whenever two or three of them are gathered together
Another little theatre comes into the world.
They are eternally leasing vacant kitchenettes
And presenting their own dramas—with Woolworth scenery.
Of course, there can be no real drama above Fourteenth Street.
If they even walked across Times Square
They'd feel that they had lost their amateur standing.
They ask you what you think of their technique,
And then wait for you to commit perjury.
They thank God that they never descended to commercialism;
They know that they'll never be appreciated—
They don't know the half of it.

And then there are the Radicals;
The Table D'Hôte Bolsheviki.
They are always in revolt about something.
Nothing has been done yet that they can wholly approve of.
Their existence is just like Heaven—
There is neither marrying nor giving in marriage.
They are forever starting magazines
And letting the Postal Authorities put the finish to them.
Their one ambition is to get themselves arrested,
So that they can come out and be Heroes.
They are always stifled—
Always longing to loose the trivial fetters of Convention,
And go far away—back to the Real—
I wish they'd get started!

I hate Bohemians;
They shatter my morale.

OUR OFFICE

An Intimate Glimpse of Vanity Fair——En Famille
A Hate Song

I hate the Office;
It cuts in on my social life.

There is the Art Department;
The Cover Hounds.
They are always explaining how the photographing machine works.
And they stand around in the green light
And look as if they had been found drowned.
They are forever discovering Great Geniuses;
They never fail to find exceptional talents
In any feminine artist under twenty-five.
Whenever the illustrations are late
The fault invariably lies with the editorial department.
They are always rushing around looking for sketches,
And writing mysterious numbers on the backs of photographs,
And cutting out pictures and pasting them into scrapbooks,
And then they say nobody can realize how hard they are worked—
They said something.

Then there is the Editorial Department;
The Literary Lights.
They are just a little holier than other people
Because they can write classics about
"'Brevity is the soul of lingerie,' said this little chemise to itself";
And "Here are five reasons for the success of the Broadway plays."
They are all full of soul;
Someone is forever stepping on their temperaments.
They are constantly having nervous breakdowns
And going away for a few weeks.
And they only come in on Saturday mornings

To hold the franchise.
They tell you what good training editorial work is.
But they don't mean to stay in it—
Some day they will be Free Lances
And write the Great Thoughts that Surge within them.
They say they only wish they could get away from the office—
That makes it unanimous.

Then there is the Fashion Department;
First Aids to Baron de Meyer.
If any garment costs less than $485
They think you ought to give it to the Belgians.
They look at everything you have on,
And then smile tolerantly
And say, "Sears, Roebuck certainly do a wonderful business,
  don't they?"
They are forever taking pictures of prominent Wild Women
Dressed as brides and kneeling at Property Altars.
And they write essays on Smart Fashions for Limited Incomes—
The sky's the limit.

There is the Boss;
The Great White Chief.
He made us what we are to-day—
I hope he's satisfied.
He has some bizarre ideas
About his employees' getting to work
At nine o'clock in the morning—
As if they were a lot of milkmen.
He has never been known to see you
When you arrive at 8:45,
But try to come in at a quarter past ten
And he will always go up in the elevator with you.
He goes to Paris on the slightest provocation

And nobody knows why he has to stay there so long.
Oh, well—
You can't expect to keep him down on the farm.

I hate the Office;
It cuts in on my social life.

ACTORS
A Hate Song

I hate Actors;
They ruin my evenings.

There are the Juveniles;
The Male Ingenues.
They always interpret the rôles of wealthy young sportsmen,
So that they can come running on in white flannels,
Carrying tennis racquets, and wearing spiked shoes.
Whenever the lights go up
They are discovered with their arms around some girl.
They wear their watches and handkerchiefs on their arms,
And they simply couldn't play a scene without their cigarette cases.
They think that the three Greatest Names in American History
Are Hart, Schaffner, and Marx.
They are constantly giving interviews to the Sunday papers
Complaining about the car-loads of mash notes they receive.
They know they have it in them to do something Really Big;
They relate how Belasco told them that they would go far—
I wish they were on their way!

There are the Movie Heroes;
The Boys Who Drove the Wild West Wild.
They are forever fading out into the sunset,
And if they can't pose for a close-up every few feet
They sue the company.
They wear their hair bobbed,
And always look as if they dressed by mail.
They were never known to lose a fight;
The whole troupe of supernumeraries hasn't a chance against them.

They are just bubbling over with animal spirits—
They are continually walking up the side of houses,
Or springing from one galloping horse to another,
Or leaping out of balloons, without parachutes.
And they love to be photographed balancing on one foot
On the extreme edge of the Grand Canyon—
Oh, that I might get behind them, just once!

Then there are the Tragedians;
The Ones Who Made Shakespeare famous.
They are always telling what they used to say to Booth.
And they talk about the old traditions
As if they had collaborated on them.
They make their positively last appearance semi-annually,
And they are just about to go on farewell tour No. 118397, Series II.
They never appear in any rôle
In which they have to wear long trousers.
If they stooped to play in any drama written after 1700,
They know that Art could never be the same.
They are forever striding around the stage in trick tempests,
Wearing aluminum armor, and waving property swords,
And shrieking at Heaven to do its worst—
I wish Heaven would kindly oblige.

And there are the Drawing-Room Stars;
The Ones That Swing a Mean Tea-Cup.
They always appear in those dramas
In which the Big Line is "No cream, please—lemon."
They interpret every emotion
By tapping the left thumb-nail with the cork-tipped cigarette.
They are invariably the best-dressed men on our stage—
Their press-agent says so himself.

They are always standing in the center of the stage
Saying cutting things about marriage;
And they hang around in property moonlight,
Making middle-aged love.
They cherish secret ambitions
To take off their cutaways and play Hamlet:
They know they could be great
If the public would only give them their just due—
If it only would!

I hate Actors;
They ruin my evenings.

BORES

A Hymn of Hate

I hate Bores;
They take the joy out of my life.

There are the Symptom Collectors.
They have tried every specialist once.
They go about, quoting what they said under ether;
They give readings from their fever-charts;
And they carry their cast-off appendixes with them, in bottles—
Just for old times' sake.
They are forever showing you X-ray photographs
Of their quaint crannies and intimate inglenooks.
They say that you can never guess what they suffer,
And then they clear up all doubts.
Every doctor tells them that their case is hopeless—
I'll say it is.

Then there are the Parlor Comedians.
They have memorized the entire series
Of history's favorite anecdotes.
They begin by saying that they just heard a new one—
Which is the funniest line in the whole story.
They go in strongly for the kind of humor
That requires special apparatus.
They will go miles to procure an exploding cigar
Or a perforated drinking-glass.
They have a repertoire of sure-fire comedy hits:
They address all waiters as "George."
And they love to call you on the telephone
And say, "This is Police Headquarters speaking."
They save up all their witticisms for you,
And tell you how everyone nearly dies at them—
Nearly dies is right.

There are the Gluttons for Business.
They started on a shoe string
And worked their way up to white spats.
They are entirely self-made,
And think that everybody is clamoring for the recipe.
Their life is an open ledger;
They tell you all the inside gossip
About invoices and bills of lading,
And illustrate their talk with diagrams
Showing their increased output throughout the Middle West.
They relate heart-rending stories
Of how they haven't had a vacation in ten years,
And how they wish they could go away for a while—
And I wish they could go away from now on.

And there are the Amateur Mediums.
They are always fooling around with the spirits.
They are constantly receiving messages from the Great Beyond
Saying Uncle Walter is well
And hopes everybody at home is the same.
They spend every night
Being warned, in dreams, of their friends' deaths.
There is nothing that they can't worm out of a ouija board.
They are so messy around the house;
They are always tipping tables
And sitting around in circles, with the lights out.
They are forever seeing things and hearing knocks,
And they just know they have clairvoyant minds—
If any.

I hate Bores;
They take the joy out of my life.

THE DRAMA
A Hymn of Hate

I hate the Drama;
It cuts in on my sleep.

There is the Clean Play;
The one you take Aunt Etta to see
After a day's sightseeing in the financial district.
The hero is the man from Back Home,
With the blameless life and the creaseless trousers—
A real rough rhinestone.
He may not be so strong on grammar,
But he loves children and sleeping outdoors.
The heroine sneers at him in Act I,
But after he has shown up the effete aristocracy,
And received news that they've struck oil
Back in the Little Marigold well,
She listens to reason.
And when the curtain falls at eleven o'clock,
They are starting out for the Great, Clean West together—
Three hours too late.

Then there is the Comedy of Manners;
The manners provide most of the comedy.
It is all about the goings-on in titled circles—
How Her Grace's handkerchief
Was found in Sir Arthur's diggings.
Tea flows like water,
Butlers are everywhere,
And there is practically no stint to the epigrams
About there being two kinds of husbands:
Your own, and the kind that is in love with you.

Everybody stands about,
Gesticulating with cucumber sandwiches,
And saying, "Oh, Lord Cyril, what a cynic you are!"
There is always a little country ingenue
Who tearfully goes back home in the last act,
Declaring that those society people are all rotten—
She said it.

There is the Farthest North performance
Of the Play That Makes You Think—
Makes you think that you should have gone to the movies.
It is translated from the Norwegian;
They might just as well give it in the original.
All the lighting is dim
So that the actors' faces can scarcely be distinguished,
Which is doubtless all for the best.
The heroine is invariably Misunderstood—
Probably because of her accent.
She is a regular little Glad Girl,
Always falling in love with an innocent bystander,
Or finding that she has married her uncle by mistake,
Or going out into the night and slamming the door.
And things come to a rousing climax
In a nice, restful suicide, or a promising case of insanity.
You tell 'em, Ibsen; you've got the Scandinavian rights.

And there is the Allegorical Drama;
It becomes as sounding brass or a tinkling symbol.
The critics can always find subtle shades of meaning in it—
The triumph of mind over Maeterlinck.
The actors play the parts
Of Light, Joy, Beauty, and Imagination,
While the audience represent Ennui and Bewilderment.

The leading character is searching for Happiness.
And after hunting through four acts, twenty-seven scenes,
And a company of three hundred, exclusive of stage-hands,
He finally discovers it at home—
Would to Heaven he had looked there in the first place!

I hate the Drama;
It cuts in on my sleep.

PARTIES
A Hymn of Hate

I hate Parties;
They bring out the worst in me.

There is the Novelty Affair,
Given by the woman
Who is awfully clever at that sort of thing.
Everybody must come in fancy dress;
There are always eleven Old-Fashioned Girls,
And fourteen Hawaiian gentlemen
Wearing the native costume
Of last season's tennis clothes, with a wreath around the neck.

The hostess introduces a series of clean, home games:
Each participant is given a fair chance
To guess the number of seeds in a cucumber,
Or thread a needle against time,
Or see how many names of wild flowers he knows.
Ice cream in trick formations,
And punch like Volstead used to make
Buoy up the players after the mental strain.
You have to tell the hostess that it's a riot,
And she says she'll just die if you don't come to her next party—
If only a guarantee went with that!

Then there is the Bridge Festival.
The winner is awarded an arts-and-crafts hearth-brush,
And all the rest get garlands of hothouse raspberries.
You cut for partners
And draw the man who wrote the game.
He won't let bygones be bygones;
After each hand
He starts getting personal about your motives in leading clubs,
And one word frequently leads to another.

At the next table
You have one of those partners
Who says it is nothing but a game, after all.
He trumps your ace
And tries to laugh it off.
And yet they shoot men like Elwell.

There is the Day in the Country;
It seems more like a week.
All the contestants are wedged into automobiles,
And you are allotted the space between two ladies
Who close in on you.
The party gets a nice early start,
Because everybody wants to make a long day of it—
They get their wish.
Everyone contributes a basket of lunch;
Each person has it all figured out
That no one else will think of bringing hard-boiled eggs.

There is intensive picking of dogwood,
And no one is quite sure what poison ivy is like;
They find out by the next day.
Things start off with a rush.
Everybody joins in the old songs,
And points out cloud effects,
And puts in a good word for the color of the grass.
But after the first fifty miles,
Nature doesn't go over so big,
And singing belongs to the lost arts.
There is a slight spurt on the homestretch,
And everyone exclaims over how beautiful the lights of the city
    look—
I'll say they do.

And there is the informal little Dinner Party;
The lowest form of taking nourishment.
The man on your left draws diagrams with a fork,

Illustrating the way he is going to have the new sun-parlor built on;
And the one on your right
Explains how soon business conditions will be better, and why.

When the more material part of the evening is over,
You have your choice of listening to the Harry Lauder records,
Or having the hostess hem you in
And show you the snapshots of the baby they took last summer.
Just before you break away,
You mutter something to the host and hostess
About sometime soon you must have them over—
Over your dead body.

I hate Parties;
They bring out the worst in me.

MOVIES

A Hymn of Hate

I hate Movies;
They lower my vitality.

There is the Great Spectacle.
Its press-agent admits
That it is the most remarkable picture ever made.
The story is taken from history,
But the scenario writer smoothes things over a little,
And makes Cleopatra Antony's wife,
Or has Salome marry John the Baptist,
So that you can bring the kiddies.
The management compiles vital statistics
About the size of the cast:
How the entire population of California
Takes part in the battle scenes;
And where the beads worn by the star would reach
If placed end to end.
The audience sits panting
And says, "Think of what it must have cost to produce it!"
Think what could have been saved by not producing it!

Then there is the Picture with Sex Appeal;
The appeal is still unanswered.
The production goes to show
That bad taste, off the screen,
Is still in its infancy.
It seeks to reveal the depths to which society has fallen,
And it proves its point.
It gives glimpses of Night Life in the Great City:
The revelers are shown wearing fancy paper hats,
And marching in lockstep around the table,
And shamelessly performing the two-step.
The characters are always driving home in motors
To the Public Library, or Senator Clark's house.

The interiors are designed
By the man who decorates dentists' waiting-rooms.
The star is a prominent vampire
Who is a nice, sweet girl when she is at home,
And supports an indulgent husband
In the style to which he has become accustomed;
The wages of sin is $3,500 a week.

There is the High Art Production:
They charge three dollars a seat for it—
That's where they get the "high."
The photography is always tricky;
The actors seem to be enveloped in a dense fog,
And that goes for the plot, too.
There is some idea of an allegorical strain running through it,
So that, whenever things are beginning to get good,
And the heroine is just about to fall,
The scene changes
To a panorama of storm clouds,
Or a still-life study of apple blossoms,
Or a view of Hong-Kong harbor by moonlight.
Every few minutes, there is a close-up of the star
Registering one of her three expressions.
The sub-titles offer positive proof
That there is a place where bad metaphors go when they die.
The critics agree unanimously
That the picture removes all doubt
As to whether movies should be classed among the arts—
Removes all doubt is right.

And there is the News of the Week.
It is assembled on the principle
That no news is good news.
It shows all the big events in current history:
The paperweight manufacturers' convention in Des Moines;
The procession of floats during Anti-Litter Week in Topeka;
And the sailors of the U.S.S. Mississippi

Grouped to form the words "E Pluribus Unum."
There is always a view of a wrecked schooner,
Enabling the pianist to oblige with "Asleep in the Deep."
When they have a chance to show a picture of a fire
They color it a mean shade of red.
Before you can get a good look at the event before you,
The scene changes to a new one
Leaving the fate of the people in the last picture hanging—
It's too good for them.

I hate Movies;
They lower my vitality.

BOOKS
A Hymn of Hate

I hate Books;
They tire my eyes.

There is the Account of Happy Days in Far Tahiti;
The booklet of South Sea Island resorts.
After his four weeks in the South Seas,
The author's English gets pretty rusty
And he has to keep dropping into the native dialect.
He implies that his greatest hardship
Was fighting off the advances of the local girls,
But the rest of the book
Was probably founded on fact.
You can pick up a lot of handy information
On how to serve *poi,*
And where the legend of the breadfruit tree got its start,
And how to take *kava* or let it alone
The author says it's the only life
And as good as promises
That sometime he is going to throw over his writing,
And go end his days with Laughing Sea-pig, the half-caste
  Knockout—
Why wait?

Then there is the Little Book of Whimsical Essays;
Not a headache in a libraryful.
The author comes right out and tells his favorite foods,
And how much he likes his pipe,
And what his walking-stick means to him—
A thrill on every page.
The essays clean up all doubt
On what the author feels when riding in the subway,
Or strolling along the Palisades.
The writer seems to be going ahead on the idea
That it isn't such a bad old world, after all;

He drowses along
Under the influence of Pollyanesthetics.
No one is ever known to buy the book;
You find it on the guest room night-table,
Or win it at a Five Hundred Party,
Or someone gives it to you for Easter
And follows that up by asking you how you liked it—
Say it with raspberries!

There is the novel of Primitive Emotions;
The Last Word in Unbridled Passions—
Last but not leashed.
The author writes about sex
As if he were the boy who got up the idea.
The hero and heroine may be running wild in the Sahara,
Or camping informally on a desert island,
Or just knocking around the city,
But the plot is always the same—
They never quite make the grade.
The man turns out to be the son of a nobleman,
Or the woman the world's greatest heiress,
And they marry and go to live together—
That can't hold much novelty for them.
It is but a question of time till the book is made into a movie,
Which is no blow to its writer.
People laugh it off
By admitting that it may not be the highest form of art;
But then, they plead, the author must live—
What's the big idea?

And then there is the Realistic Novel;
Five hundred pages without a snicker.
It is practically an open secret
That the book is two dollars' worth of the author's own experiences,
And that if he had not been through them,
It would never have been written,
Which would have been all right with me.

It presents a picture of quiet family life—
Of how little Rosemary yearns to knife Grandpa,
And Father wishes Mother were cold in her grave,
And Bobby wants to marry his big brother.
The author's idea of action
Is to make one of his characters spill the cereal.
The big scene of the book
Is the heroine's decision to make over her old taffeta.
All the characters are in a bad way;
They have a lot of trouble with their suppressions.
The author is constantly explaining that they are all being stifled—
I wish to God he'd give them the air!

I hate Books;
They tire my eyes.

THE YOUNGER SET
A Hymn of Hate

I hate the Younger Set;
They harden my arteries.

There are the Boy Authors;
The ones who are going to put *belles lettres* on their feet.
Every night before they go to sleep
They kneel down and ask H. L. Mencken
To bless them and make them good boys.
They are always carrying volumes with home-cut pages,
And saying that after all, there is only one Remy de Gourmont;
Which doesn't get any dissension out of me.
They shrink from publicity
As you or I would
From the gift of a million dollars.
At the drop of a hat
They will give readings from their works—
In department stores,
Or grain elevators,
Or ladies' dressing-rooms.
It is pretty hard to get them to show you their work;
Sometimes you even have to ask them to.
They are constantly backing you into corners,
And asking you to glance over some little things
That they just dashed off in a spare year—
Read 'em and weep!

Then there are the Male Flappers;
The Usual Dancing Men.
They can drink one straight Orange Pekoe after another,
And you'd never know that they had had a thing.
Four débutante parties a night is bogie for them,
And their talk is very small indeed.
They never claimed to go so big at a desk,
But they can balance a plate of chicken salad, a cup of bouillon,

And a guest-room-size napkin,
And make gestures with the other hand.
They are mean boys when the orchestra starts;
They work in so many wise steps
That you can't tell whether it's a waltz or a track-meet.
No one can tie them, at a charity entertainment;
They say they have often been told
That with their talent
And the way they can wear clothes
They are simply wasting time on the amateur stage—
I can't give them any argument on that one.

There are the Black Sheep;
The Boys with the Nasty Records.
They are always giving you glimpses of the darker side of life—
Telling you what time they got to bed yesterday morning
And how many people passed out cold,
And where they went from there.
They virtually admit
That if they ever turned over a new leaf
The bootlegging industry would go straight to smash.
They are so inured to alcohol,
That as soon as they've had one cocktail,
They want to go right out and address the Senate.
They are always consulting little red notebooks,
Containing names, telephone numbers, and authors' notes,
And it is an open secret that they have met an actress.
They tell you they know they are going the pace that kills,
And then they laugh bitterly,
And say, "But what does it matter?"—
They took the words right out of my mouth.

And there are the Heavy Thinkers;
The Gluttons for Head-Work.
They have got up a lot of novel ideas
About everybody having a right to live his own life,
And about marriage being just a few words

Muttered over you by a minister.
They say that there may be
Some Supreme Force back of the universe;
They will look into that when they get the time.
Just stand back and give them room,
And they will drop the conventions for the count.
They are pretty low in their minds about America;
They hint that its civilization
Is practically plucking at the coverlet,
And that the Other Side is the only place for intellectuals—
Bon voyage!

I hate the Younger Set;
They harden my arteries.

SUMMER RESORTS

A Hymn of Hate

I hate Summer Resorts;
They ruin my vacation.

There is the Seaside Hotel.
The booklets say that it is right on the water,
And they aren't much over quarter-of-a-mile out of the way.
You are never at a loss for something to do;
You can go down by the waves
And watch the gentleman in sneakers
Trying out his Little Admiral water-wings,
Or you can sit on the porch
And listen to the lady in the next rocker
Explain that this is the first Summer she has ever been to a place
Where the rates were less than fifteen dollars a day.
There is always lots of excitement down on the beach—
Group photographs are constantly being taken.
And posses are being formed to find the person or persons
Who took the garters out of bathhouse number 38
And if you play your cards right,
You may be able to find a dead horseshoe crab.
The more highly-strung guests take you aside and tell you
How much the water means to them.
And how they wish they could stay there beside it for ever and ever—
Good here!

And there is the place where you can get Back to Nature,
Or even farther.
The house was built
When electric lights were regarded as Edison's Folly,
And the surface of plumbing has only been scratched,
And the proprietor hasn't got around to making any changes.

You can tell the tennis court by the net:
Otherwise you would think it was an old-fashioned rock garden
Planted with all the flowers mentioned in Shakespeare's works,
And if you want to play golf,
You will find a course three counties to the left.
The guests are like one big family—
Just like that.
You sit at the table with a lady from Montclair
Who gives talks on the trouble that Junior has had with his tonsils.
Everyone says how restful it all is,
And how it seems as if the city must be a thousand miles away—
It's an under-estimate.

There is the Synthetic Newport;
Luke-warm Dog!
The life is pretty fairly speedy;
Many of the young married set inhale right out in public.
Silver frequently changes hands after the bridge games.
And you'd almost think the cocktails were made of the real stuff—
That goes for the whole works.
Extra-mural affection is generally indulged in:
If you sit down next to your own husband,
It's all over the country club that you are insanely jealous of him.
The revelers have their intellectual side, too;
There is scarcely one of them that hasn't read "The Sheik,"
They are the first to concede that they are hitting things up.
They say that there won't be a thing left of them
If they keep up the pace all Summer—
Stay with 'em, boys!

And then there is the Mountain Resort;
The Home of American Scenery.
You can go yodling up Old Baldy—
Five hundred feet above sea level—
Or you can collect postcard views of Lovers' Leap,
To pass around among your friends on Winter evenings.
You can't conscientiously call it a Summer
Until you get a good, clear day
When you can figure out Washington's profile in the peaks—
You can see a better one on a two-cent stamp
Even when it's raining.
The gossip on the porch keeps you right on the edge of your seat;
One transient tells how he is pretty sure he saw a trout jump,
And hardly has the uproar died down
Before someone else claims to have found some genuine
  maidenhair fern.
The guests are seldom without a kind word for the landscape,
And they have nothing but praise to offer the air—
It's all theirs.

I hate Summer Resorts;
They ruin my vacation.

REFORMERS

A Hymn of Hate

I hate Reformers;
They raise my blood pressure.

There are the Prohibitionists;
The Fathers of Bootlegging.
They made us what we are to-day—
I hope they're satisfied.
They can prove that the Johnstown flood,
And the blizzard of 1888,
And the destruction of Pompeii
Were all due to alcohol.
They have it figured out
That anyone who would give a gin daisy a friendly look
Is just wasting time out of jail,
And anyone who would stay under the same roof
With a bottle of Scotch
Is right in line for a cozy seat in the electric chair.
They fixed things all up pretty for us;
Now that they have dried up the country,
You can hardly get a drink unless you go in and order one.
They are in a nasty state over this light wines and beer idea;
They say that lips that touch liquor
Shall never touch wine.
They swear that the Eighteenth Amendment
Shall be improved upon
Over their dead bodies—
Fair enough!

Then there are the Suppressors of Vice;
The Boys Who Made the Name of Cabell a Household Word.
Their aim is to keep art and letters in their place;
If they see a book
Which does not come right out and say
That the doctor brings babies in his little black bag,

Or find a painting of a young lady
Showing her without her rubbers,
They call out the militia.
They have a mean eye for dirt;
They can find it
In a copy of "What Katy Did at School,"
Or a snapshot of Aunt Bessie in bathing at Sandy Creek,
Or a picture postcard of Moonlight in Bryant Park.
They are always running around suppressing things,
Beginning with their desires.
They get a lot of excitement out of life—
They are constantly discovering
The New Rabelais
Or the Twentieth Century Hogarth.
Their leader is regarded
As the representative of Comstock here on earth.
How does that song of Tosti's go?
"Good-bye, Sumner, good-bye, good-bye."

There are the Movie Censors,
The motion picture is still in its infancy—
They are the boys who keep it there.
If the film shows a party of clubmen tossing off ginger ale,
Or a young bride dreaming over tiny garments,
Or Douglas Fairbanks kissing Mary Pickford's hand,
They cut out the scene
And burn it in the public square.
They fix up all the historical events
So that their own mothers wouldn't know them.
They make Du Barry Mrs. Louis Fifteenth,
And show that Anthony and Cleopatra were like brother and sister,
And announce Salome's engagement to John the Baptist,
So that the audiences won't go and get ideas in their heads.
They insist that Sherlock Holmes is made to say,
"Quick, Watson, the crochet needle!"
And the state pays them for it.

They say they are going to take the sin out of cinema
If they perish in the attempt—
I wish to God they would!

And then there are the All-American Crabs;
The Brave Little Band that is Against Everything.
They have got up the idea
That things are not what they were when Grandma was a girl.
They say that they don't know what we're coming to,
As if they had just written the line.
They are always running a temperature
Over the modern dances,
Or the new skirts,
Or the goings-on of the younger set.
They can barely hold themselves in
When they think of the menace of the drama;
They seem to be going ahead under the idea
That everything but the Passion Play
Was written by Avery Hopwood.
They will never feel really themselves
Until every theatre in the country is razed.
They are forever signing petitions
Urging that cigarette-smokers should be deported,
And that all places of amusement should be closed on Sunday
And kept closed all week.
They take everything personally;
They go about shaking their heads,
And sighing, "It's all wrong, it's all wrong"—
They said it.

I hate Reformers;
They raise my blood pressure.

WIVES

A Hymn of Hate

I hate Wives;
Too many people have them.

There are the Splendid Housekeepers;
The Girls Who Shake a Mean Furnace.
Give them a darning-egg, and a box of assorted hooks and eyes,
And they wouldn't change places with Lady Mountbatten.
They keep you right on the edge of your chair
With stories about the stoppage in the kitchen drain,
And how impudent Delia was about those new aprons,
And how they have every reason to believe
That the laundress is taking soap home to her folks.
For comedy relief
They relate how they wise-cracked the butcher
When he told them veal cutlets had gone up.
Their books are their best friends;
They love to browse in "Thirty Pretty Ways to Cook Cauliflower"
Or "Two Hundred Daring Stitches in Filet Crochet."
They can't see why people should want to go out nights;
Their idea of whooping things up
Is to sit by the sewing-table, and listen for Junior's croup.
They are always making second-hand puddings,
Or seeing whether the blue vase doesn't look better on the piano
Than it did on the bookcase.
Oh, well—
It keeps them out of the open air.

Then there are the Veteran Sirens;
The Ones Who Are Wedded, but What of It?
They can take their husbands, or let them alone—
But not in the order named.
Any unmarried man above the age of Jackie Coogan
They regard as All Theirs.
They are constantly helping to fix up bachelor apartments,

Or visiting the male sick, with jars of beef tea,
Or picking out oddities in neckwear for their Boy Friends.
If any man they know goes and gets married,
They feel that they have grounds for a breach of promise suit.
They are always talking in low voices over the telephone,
And carefully dropping letters out of their hand-bags,
And going around full of smiling mystery
About where they are having tea.
They say they wish to goodness
They could have a moment to themselves;
They'd give anything if some nice girl would come along
And take some of their admirers off their hands—
Try and get them!

There are the Drooping Lilies;
The Girls Who Could Have Married That Man with All That Money.
They are always parking a secret sorrow,
And you must guess what the unshed tears are all about.
Their husbands may look normal in public,
But they are Little Better than Animals in the home.
You have no idea what they have to put up with—
Their husbands dance with Another Woman
Twice in the same evening,
Or won't read anything but the newspapers,
Or simply refuse to touch spinach in any form.
If they could only bring themselves
To write down what they have been through
It would be the biggest day that Literature ever saw.
Everyone tells them they might have gone on the stage
And become the toast of the town,
Or put the movies on a paying basis,
Or sent the interior decorating business for a loop—
And here they are—yoked to a lot of Clods!
Things may looks pretty black for them now,
But some day,
Some day they know that they will get their due—
I hope to God they will!

And then there are the Regular Little Pals;
More Like Friends than Wives.
They go everywhere with their husbands
Just to hold the franchise.
You find them up at the Polo Grounds
Asking which is the Yankee eleven;
Or on the golf links
Making a fifth in a Sunday morning foursome;
Or lending a feminine touch to a poker game—
Going ahead on the idea that a straight is better than a flush.
They are a big help in their husbands' business affairs;
They are always dropping in at the office
For little surprise visits.
They smile happily at you
And ask you what their husbands would ever do without them—
I'll give you three guesses!

I hate Wives;
Too many people have them.

HUSBANDS

A Hymn of Hate

I hate Husbands;
They narrow my scope.

There are the Home Bodies;
The Boys for Whom the Marriage Idea Was Got Up.
If it wasn't for them
The suburbs would have shut down long ago.
Give them a hammer and a mouthful of tacks,
And you'll never have to worry about where they spend their
   evenings.
Their business cuts in horribly on their night life:
They can hardly wait to rush back to the love nest
And do their stuff.
Some big undertaking is always on their minds—
If it isn't bobbing the hedge,
It's putting up the new shelf for the preserves.
They take you off into corners,
And tell you the latest good one that's going the rounds
About how much they saved by chopping the kindling wood
   themselves.
They are seldom mistaken for Rudolph Valentino;
The militia has not yet been called out to keep the women back.
They dress right up to their rôle;
The neckties launder without a scruple,
The collars were designed when Gramercy Square was considered
   up-town,
And the suits were tailored by the visiting seamstress.
It isn't as if they never burned up the White Lights;
Every wedding anniversary
They shoot the works
And take the wife to dinner at Ye Golden Glow Waffle Shoppe.
They are always trying to sell matrimony to the old school friends.
Their big contention is

That there's nothing like it—
Where's the argument?

Then there are the He-Men;
The Masters in Their Own Homes.
The news about the equality of the sexes
Hasn't got around to them yet.
Their conception of the perfect woman
Is one who sews the buttons on before they come off.
They wouldn't give Helen of Troy a second look
If they heard she wasn't so snappy at darning socks.
They are the life of the household;
If the eggs are done longer than three minutes,
They don't speak until the next month.
If the helpmate is ten minutes late getting home
She has to show a letter from her pastor.
They are great boys on a party;
Any time any one else asks the wife to dance,
They want to plead the Unwritten Law.
Their notion of feminine repartee
Is "Yes, dear, of course you're right."
They say that if things ever got to the point
Where they were not the acknowledged Head of the House,
They would never show their faces again—
That's an idea, too.

There are the Steppers-Out;
Married, but What's That between Friends?
They tell you that the wife is a great little woman,
And that closes the subject.
They show you how tall Junior is with one hand,
And try to guess your weight with the other.
Their conquests are a dark secret;
They don't tell a soul until after they have been introduced
They are always looking for new talent;
Can they help it if the rumor got out
That all the last year's Follies Girls

Are so many withered violets to them?
They may always be found on dance floors
Tiring out the flappers;
Or in dark corners
Telling fortunes by palmistry;
Or leaning up against tea tables,
Crazed with cinnamon toast.
Try to tell them what devils they are,
And all the thanks you get for it
Is their lifelong friendship.
They may be a bit gay,
But there is no more harm in them
Than there is in Mussolini.
They explain that some temperaments can stand restraint,
But as for them,
Give them liberty or give them death—
I wish to God they'd leave the decision with me!

And then there are the Gloom Kings;
The Gluttons for Sympathy.
They are the human Einstein theories—
Nobody at home understands them.
They have a rough time getting their stuff across;
The wife may be all very well in her way,
But when it comes to Understanding,
She can't make the grade.
If only they had married some rising young mind-reader,
They could have saved themselves a lot of trouble.
They wear cynical little smiles,
And go around giving impersonations of Disillusionment.
They tell you that of course they can never say anything,
But sometimes they almost think you know—
Which is a big estimate.
You can see that they wish the wife all the luck in the world
By the way they relate the plans for what they would do
If they were ever free.

They like to toy with the idea
That they will just drop quietly Out of Things some day;
They laugh bitterly,
And say everybody would be better off if they did—
The ayes have it!

I hate Husbands;
They narrow my scope.

COLLEGE BOYS

A Hymn of Hate

I hate College Boys;
They get under my feet.

There are the Boy Butterflies;
The Haberdashers' Livelihood.
Society would be on the rocks without them;
They are as much a part of every tea
As the watercress sandwiches.
They list all the débutantes
In Grades A, B, and C,
And proceed accordingly.
Once they get into their stride,
The Opposite Sex hasn't a prayer.
They are great boys in the moonlight,
And if there were ever a contest in sitting out dances
They could enter at scratch.
They are always dropping lavender envelopes,
Or returning photographs,
Or leaving word that they are not at home
In case a woman's voice asks for them on the telephone.
They wish to God the girls would leave them alone—
That falls right in with my plans.

Then there are the Athletes;
All Full of Red Blood, or What Have You?
They eat their meat just this side of raw,
They are constantly flinging windows open,
And they can hardly wrench themselves out of their cold showers.
They may be the Biceps Kings,
But if you sneak up on them suddenly,
And ask them who discovered America,
They have to rack their memories.
They are all due to make a big name in the business world;

Look at the way they can tear telephone books in half,
And bend silver quarters,
And chin themselves seventy-five consecutive times.
When football comes into the conversation,
It turns out that they are the boys who wrote the rules.
They are always doing something helpful—
You find them on the bathing beaches
Forming human pyramids;
Or on country club verandas
Holding rocking-chairs out at arm's length;
Or standing on their hands
In some lucky girl's parlor.
It's rough that they have to be cramped up in cities;
Way up in the clean, cold, silent out-of-doors,
That's where they ought to be—
And now!

There are the Hot Puppies;
The High-Place Hitters.
They may be young as years go,
But they are old in night life.
You would never dream of the wicked things that go on
If they didn't take pity
And clear it all up for you.
They have piled up a nasty record for themselves;
Try and hear it without blushing.
They tear the town wide open
Until nearly eleven o'clock at night,
They talk right back to policemen.
And when it comes to alcohol,
They imply that they can take it or let it alone—
Reading from left to right.
They concede that they are just about as scarlet as they come,
And they perform a mean laugh,
And say that terrible isn't the word for them—
I heard different.

And there are the Heavy Thinkers;
The Boys That Know the Answers.
Bring up any subject at all
And they'll be glad to set you right on it.
I forget what they go to college for:
It can't be education,
Because they had all that under control years ago.
They don't go so big on a dance floor,
But when the party gets loose,
And Greek irregular verbs are being bandied about,
They are the hit of the evening.
They can hold their audiences spellbound;
If it isn't the latest trigonometry problem that's going the rounds,
Then it's the good one the boys are telling
About the advantages of the parliamentary form of government.
If they were to appear in public
Without a book under their arm
They would feel as if they had come out without their socks.
They seldom hear, when they are spoken to;
It's because their heads are so full
Of little gems of old-world philosophy—
You know the old crack:
Nietzsche abhors a vacuum.

I hate College Boys;
They get under my feet.

Index of First Lines

Poem and Free Verse Source List

Dorothy Parker was born in 1893. She published most of her verse in various newspapers and magazines from 1915 to 1944. She collected most of these items into three original compilations: *Enough Rope* (*Rope*) (published 1926); *Sunset Gun* (*Gun*) (1928); and *Death and Taxes* (*Taxes*) (1931). In 1936 she collected most, but not all, of the items that originally appeared in *Rope, Gun,* and *Taxes* into the single-volume *Not So Deep as a Well* (*Well*). In 1944 she incorporated the full contents of *Well,* with one more item, into the *Portable Dorothy Parker* (*Portable*), which also included other material. She died in 1967.

In 1996 Scribner published *Not Much Fun* (*Fun*), the fourth original compilation of Mrs. Parker's poems and free verses; that is, all the previously uncollected items that the editor subjectively determined were poems, or free verses, that were properly attributed to Mrs. Parker. Mrs. Parker occasionally changed the titles of items when she compiled them; the editor of *Fun* did likewise.

This new second edition of *Not Much Fun* (*Fun 2*) (2009) revises and updates the 1996 *Fun* first edition. This 2009 edition includes all the items contained in the 1996 *Fun* except "Day-Dreams," a previously collected item (in *Rope*) that inadvertently appeared in the 1996 *Fun*; it also supplies four very old "new" items that do not appear in the text of the 1996 *Fun* ("Pollyanna Gets the Air," "Blurb," "Pecking Order [or 'Eggs Tempore']," and "Hymn of Hate: Reformers"), and the full text of another item ("The Passionate Screenwriter to His Love") of which only a small fragment appears in the 1996 *Fun*.

This "Poem and Free Verse Source List" supplies publication information for every item that appears in the seven compilations described above (*Rope, Gun, Taxes, Well, Portable, Fun,* and *Fun 2*), not only those contained in this book (*Fun 2*); it also lists where and when each item was first published, any alternate titles under which it was later compiled, and the compilation(s) in which it appeared.

Also note: (1) in instances where a date of creation that substantially precedes publication can be established, the earlier date is cited; and (2) to avoid unnecessary clutter, *Fun 2* is cited below only for the items that do not also appear in *Fun,* and *Portable* only for the item that does not also appear in *Well*.

The list follows this format: Item Title [New Title(s) in Compilation(s)] [*Compilation(s)*]; then First Published Source, Date, Page.

Poem (or "Modernist Verse")	Source, Date, Page
Any Porch (*Fun*)	*Vanity Fair,* Sep 1915, 32*[1]
The Bridge Fiend (*Fun*)	*Vanity Fair,* Jan 1916, 118*[1]
A Musical Comedy Thought (*Fun*)	*Vanity Fair,* Jun 1916, 126*[1]
The Gunman and the Débutante (*Fun*)	*Vanity Fair,* Oct 1916, 120*[1]
The Lady in Back (*Fun*)	*Vogue,* Nov 15, 1916, 128*[1]
Oh, Look—I Can Do It, Too (*Fun*)	*Vanity Fair,* Dec 1918, 48
Letter to Robert Benchley (*Fun*)	**Unpublished, Sep 1920**
Our Own Home Talent (*Fun*)	*Life,* Sep 30, 1920, 527
With Best Wishes (*Fun*)	*Life,* Dec 2, 1920, 1039
Invictus (*Fun*)	*Life,* Feb 3, 1921, 160
Song of the Open Country (*Fun*)	*Life,* Apr 7, 1921, 487
The Passionate Freudian to His Love (*Fun*)	*Life,* Apr 28, 1921, 596
Love Song (*Fun*)	*Life,* Jun 30, 1921, 933
Idyl (*Fun*)	*Life,* Jul 7, 1921, 3
To My Dog (*Fun*)	*Life,* Jul 28, 1921, 8
Absence (*Fun*)	*Life,* Aug 18, 1921, 1
Lyric (*Fun*)	*Life,* Sep 15, 1921, 3
Song for the First of the Month (*Fun*)	*Life,* Oct 6, 1921, 3
Fulfilment (*Fun*)	*Life,* Oct 27, 1921, 1
Lynn Fontanne (*Fun*)	*Life,* Nov 24, 1921, 3
To Marjorie Rambeau (*Fun*)	*Life,* Dec 8, 1921, 7
Christmas, 1921 (*Fun*)	*Life,* Dec 15, 1921, 3

Marilyn Miller (*Fun*)	*Life,* Dec 15, 1921, 5
Fragment (*Fun*)	*Life,* Jan 12, 1922, 1
Figures in Popular Literature (FPL): The Sheik (*Fun*)	*Life,* Jan 19, 1922, 24
FPL: The Flapper (*Fun*)	*Life,* Jan 26, 1922, 22
Chantey (*Fun*)	*Life,* Feb 2, 1922, 1
Moral Tales for the Young [1] (*Fun*)	*Life,* Feb 9, 1922, 11
Valentine (V): Princess Mary and Viscount Lascelles (*Fun*)	*Life,* Feb 16, 1922, 16
V: David Wark Griffith (*Fun*)	*Life,* Feb 16, 1922, 16
V: David Belasco (*Fun*)	*Life,* Feb 16, 1922, 16
V: Calvin Coolidge (*Fun*)	*Life,* Feb 16, 1922, 16
V: Dr. Frank Crane (*Fun*)	*Life,* Feb 16, 1922, 17
V: Avery Hopwood (*Fun*)	*Life,* Feb 16, 1922, 17
V: Florenz Ziegfeld (*Fun*)	*Life,* Feb 16, 1922, 17
V: John Wanamaker (*Fun*)	*Life,* Feb 16, 1922, 17
Nocturne (*Rope, Well*)	*Life,* Mar 2, 1922, 4
The Far-Sighted Muse (*Fun*)	*Life,* Mar 9, 1922, 3
FPL: The Drab Heroine (*Fun*)	*Life,* Mar 9, 1922, 22
Paging Saint Patrick (*Fun*)	*Life,* Mar 16, 1922, 3
Mood (*Fun*)	*Life,* Mar 23, 1922, 5
Triolets (*Fun*)	*Life,* Mar 23, 1922, 12
FPL: The Western Hero (*Fun*)	*Life,* Mar 23, 1922, 24
To Myrtilla, on Easter Day (*Fun*)	*Life,* Apr 6, 1922, 5

Rondeau Redoublé (*Rope, Well*)	*Life,* Apr 13, 1922, 3
FPL: The Glad Girl (*Fun*)	*Life,* Apr 13, 1922, 24
Plea (*Rope, Well*)	*Life,* Apr 27, 1922, 3
FPL: The Boy Savant (*Fun*)	*Life,* Apr 27, 1922, 24
Moral Tales for the Young [2] (*Fun*)	*Life,* May 4, 1922, 7
Poem in the American Manner (*Fun*)	*Life,* May 11, 1922, 9
Thoughts (*Fun*)	*Life,* May 18, 1922, 1
Fantasy (*Fun*)	*Life,* Jun 1, 1922, 19
Renunciation (*Rope, Well*)	*Life,* Jun 1, 1922, 21
Men I'm Not Married To (*Fun*)	*Saturday Evening Post,* Jun 17, 1922, 13
Woodland Song (*Fun*)	*Life,* Jun 22, 1922, 1
Pollyanna Gets the Air (*Fun 2* only)	*Life,* Jun 22, 1922, 4*[5]
Rondeau [1] (*Fun*)	*Life,* Jun 22, 1922, 9
Day-Dreams (*Rope* only)	*Life,* Jun 29, 1922, 1
FPL: The Great Lover (*Fun*)	*Life,* Jun 29, 1922, 22
Folk Song [Folk Tune] (*Rope* only)	*Life,* Jul 20, 1922, 23
Rosemary [1] (*Fun*)	*Saturday Evening Post,* Jul 29, 1922, 16*[3]
Song [1] (*Fun*)	*Saturday Evening Post,* Jul 29, 1922, 46
Grandfather Said It (*Fun*)	*Saturday Evening Post,* Aug 19, 1922, 22
Monody (*Fun*)	*Saturday Evening Post,* Sep 9, 1922, 28*[3]
Somewhat Delayed Spring Song (*Fun*)	*Saturday Evening Post,* Sep 30, 1922, 105
Song in a Minor Key (*Rope* only)	*Life,* Oct 5, 1922, 7

Finis (*Rope* only)	*Life,* Jun 14, 1923, 7
Triolet [2] (*Fun*)	*Saturday Evening Post,* Jun 16, 1923, 105
Ballade of a Not Insupportable Loss (*Fun*)	*Life,* Jun 21, 1923, 9
Song of a Hopeful Heart (*Fun*)	*Life,* Jan 3, 1924, 12
Verse for a Certain Dog (*Rope,Well*)	*Life,* Jan 31, 1924, 3
Song [4] (*Fun*)	*Life,* Mar 20, 1924, 11
Song for an April Dusk (*Fun*)	*Life,* Apr 24, 1924, 20
Ballade at Thirty-five [Ballade at Thirty-Five] (*Rope,Well*)	*Life,* Jun 26, 1924, 12
Portrait of a Lady [A Certain Lady] (*Rope,Well*)	*Life,* Aug 7, 1924, 3
Rosemary [2] (*Fun*)	*Life,* Aug 14, 1924, 6
Ballade of a Complete Flop (*Fun*)	*Life,* Sep 18, 1924, 3
Ballade of Big Plans (*Rope* only)	NY *World,* Sep 22, 1924, 11
Now at Liberty (*Rope,Well*)	*Life,* Oct 2, 1924, 9
Folk Song (*Fun*)	*Life,* Oct 16, 1924, 7
Love Song (*Rope,Well*)	*Life,* Oct 23, 1924, 20
Lullaby (*Rope,Well*)	*Life,* Nov 27, 1924, 7
Light of Love (*Rope,Well*)	NY *World,* Dec 27, 1924, 7
Song of Perfect Propriety (*Rope,Well*)	*Life,* Jan 22, 1925, 12
Balto (*Fun*)	*Life,* Feb 26, 1925, 15
Cassandra Drops Into Verse (*Fun*)	*New Yorker,* Feb 28, 1925, 5
I Shall Come Back (*Rope,Well*)	NY *World,* Mar 20, 1925, 13
Biographies (*Rope* only)	*Life,* Apr 9, 1925, 10

A Dream Lies Dead (*Gun, Well*)	NY *World,* May 9, 1925, 11
Story of Mrs. W— (*Rope, Well*)	NY *World,* Jun 13, 1925, 11
Little Song [A Well-Worn Story] (*Rope, Well*)	NY *World,* Jun 26, 1925, 11
Braggart (*Rope, Well*)	NY *World,* Jun 30, 1925, 11
Epitaph (*Rope, Well*)	*New Yorker,* Jul 18, 1925, 7
Threnody (*Rope, Well*)	NY *World,* Jul 31, 1925, 11
Epitaph for a Darling Lady (*Rope, Well*)	NY *World,* Aug 3, 1925, 11
Some Beautiful Letters (SBL): Observation (*Rope, Well*)	NY *World,* Aug 16, 1925, V-3
SBL: Social Note (*Rope, Well*)	NY *World,* Aug 16, 1925, V-3
SBL: News Item (*Rope, Well*)	NY *World,* Aug 16, 1925, V-3
SBL: Interview (*Rope, Well*)	NY *World,* Aug 16, 1925, V-3
SBL: Comment (*Rope, Well*)	NY *World,* Aug 16, 1925, V-3
SBL: Resume [Résumé] (*Rope, Well*)	NY *World,* Aug 16, 1925, V-3
Convalescent (*Rope, Well*)	NY *World,* Aug 18, 1925, 13
Wail (*Rope, Well*)	*Life,* Aug 20, 1925, 3
Testament (*Rope, Well*)	NY *World,* Aug 20, 1925, 11
Recurrence (*Rope, Well*)	NY *World,* Aug 28, 1925, 11
August (*Rope, Well*)	NY *World,* Aug 29, 1925, 9
Hearthside (*Rope, Well*)	NY *World,* Sep 13, 1925, V-3
Rainy Night (*Rope, Well*)	*New Yorker,* Sep 26, 1925, 10
The Satin Dress (*Rope, Well*)	NY *World,* Jan 20, 1926, 13

Paths (*Rope, Well*)	*Vanity Fair,* Feb 1926, 44
The Trifler (*Rope, Well*)	*Vanity Fair,* Feb 1926, 44
I Know I Have Been Happiest (*Rope, Well*)	*Vanity Fair,* Mar 1926, 70
The Small Hours (*Rope, Well*)	*Vanity Fair,* Apr 1926, 64
Meeting-Place (*Fun*)	*Vanity Fair,* Apr 1926, 64
Songs Just a Little Off Key (SJLOK): Portrait of the Artist (*Rope, Well*)	*Life,* Apr 8, 1926, 11
SJLOK: Experience (*Rope, Well*)	*Life,* Apr 8, 1926, 11
SJLOK: Inscription for the Ceiling of a Bedroom (*Rope, Well*)	*Life,* Apr 8, 1926, 11
SJLOK: Unfortunate Coincidence (*Rope, Well*)	*Life,* Apr 8, 1926, 11
SJLOK: Philosophy (*Rope, Well*)	*Life,* Apr 8, 1926, 11
SJLOK: Autobiography (*Rope* only)	*Life,* Apr 8, 1926, 11
Song of Americans Resident in France (*Fun*)	*New Yorker,* May 1, 1926, 18
Rhyme of an Involuntary Violet (*Fun*)	*New Yorker,* May 15, 1926, 16
A Very Short Song (*Rope, Well*)	*Vanity Fair,* Aug 1926, 44
Songs Slightly Tainted by Sex (SSTS): Symptom Recital (*Rope, Well*)	*Life,* Aug 19, 1926, 9
SSTS: Song of One of the Girls (*Rope, Well*)	*Life,* Aug 19, 1926, 9
SSTS: Men (*Rope, Well*)	*Life,* Aug 19, 1926, 9
SSTS: Verse Reporting Late Arrival at a Conclusion (*Rope* only)	*Life,* Aug 19, 1926, 9
SSTS: The Burned Child (*Rope, Well*)	*Life,* Aug 19, 1926, 9

SSTS: For an Unknown Lady (*Rope, Well*)	*Life*, Aug 19, 1926, 9
SSTS: General Review of the Sex Situation (*Rope, Well*)	*Life*, Aug 19, 1926, 9
Neither Bloody Nor Bowed (*Rope, Well*)	*Life*, Aug 26, 1926, 5
A Portrait (*Rope, Well*)	*Vanity Fair*, Sep 1926, 58
The Thin Edge (*Rope, Well*)	*Life*, Sep 2, 1926, 13
Chant for Dark Hours (*Rope, Well*)	*Life*, Sep 9, 1926, 5
Songs of a Markedly Personal Nature (SMPN): Somebody's Story [Somebody's Song] (*Rope, Well*)	*New Yorker*, Sep 25, 1926, 21
SMPN: Prophetic Heart [Prophetic Soul] (*Rope, Well*)	*New Yorker*, Sep 25, 1926, 21
SMPN: Questions, to Date Unanswered [On Being a Woman] (*Gun, Well*)	*New Yorker*, Sep 25, 1926, 21
SMPN: Conjecture [Theory] (*Gun, Well*)	*New Yorker*, Sep 25, 1926, 21
SMPN: De Profundis (*Rope, Well*)	*New Yorker*, Sep 25, 1926, 21
SMPN: Indian Summer (*Rope, Well*)	*New Yorker*, Sep 25, 1926, 21
The Leal (*Rope, Well*)	*Life*, Sep 30, 1926, 13
The New Love (*Rope, Well*)	*Vanity Fair*, Oct 1926, 73
Godspeed (*Rope, Well*)	*Life*, Oct 7, 1926, 8
The Dark Girl's Rhyme (*Rope, Well*)	NY *World*, Oct 7, 1926, 15
The White Lady (*Rope, Well*)	NY *World*, Oct 8, 1929, 15
Faute de Mieux [Faut de Mieux] (*Rope, Well*)	*Life*, Oct 14, 1926, 15
The Trusting Heart (*Gun, Well*)	*Life*, Oct 21, 1926, 17

Fighting Words (*Rope, Well*)	*Life,* Oct 28, 1926, 13
The Immortals (*Rope, Well*)	*Vanity Fair,* Nov 1926, 83
Inventory (*Rope, Well*)	*Life,* Nov 11, 1926, 12
The Temptress (*Fun*)	*Life,* Nov 18, 1926, 15
To Elspeth (*Fun*)	NY *World,* Nov 24, 1926, 15
For a Much Too Unfortunate Lady [To a Much Too Unfortunate Lady] (*Rope, Well*)	*Life,* Dec 2, 1926, 28
Words of Comfort [Words of Comfort to Be Scratched on a Mirror] (*Rope, Well*)	*Life,* Dec 2, 1926, 45
Pictures in the Smoke (*Rope, Well*)	*Life,* Dec 9, 1926, 9
A Fairly Sad Story [A Fairly Sad Tale] (*Gun, Well*)	*New Yorker,* Jan 8, 1927, 20
Verses in the Night (VIN): Honeymoon (*Gun* only)	NY *World,* Feb 18, 1927, 13
VIN: Triolet (*Gun* only)	NY *World,* Feb 18, 1927, 13
VIN: Melange for the Unknown George (*Gun* only)	NY *World,* Feb 18, 1927, 13
Songs Not Encumbered by Reticence (SNER): The Enemy [Mortal Enemy] (*Gun, Well*)	*New Yorker,* Feb 19, 1927, 28
Partial Comfort (*Gun, Well*)	*Life,* Feb 24, 1927, 5
SNER: Fulfilment [Fulfillment] (*Gun, Well*)	*New Yorker,* Feb 26, 1927, 24
SNER: To a Favorite Granddaughter [For a Favorite Granddaughter] (*Gun, Well*)	*New Yorker,* Mar 5, 1927, 26
When We Were Very Sore (*Fun*)	NY *World,* Mar 10, 1927, 15

SNER: Afternoon (*Gun, Well*)   New Yorker, Mar 12, 1927, 28

SNER: Three-Volume Novel
[Two-Volume Novel] (*Gun, Well*)   New Yorker, Mar 19, 1927, 28

SNER: Healed (*Gun, Well*)   New Yorker, Mar 19, 1927, 28

SNER: Superfluous Advice
(*Gun, Well*)   New Yorker, Mar 19, 1927, 28

There Was One (*Gun, Well*)   NY World, Mar 23, 1927, 15

The Accursed (*Fun*)   Life, Mar 24, 1927, 13

SNER: The Second Oldest Story
(*Gun, Well*)   New Yorker, Mar 26, 1927, 26

Swan Song (*Gun* only)   New Yorker, Apr 2, 1927, 23

Thought for a Sunshiny Morning
(*Gun, Well*)   New Yorker, Apr 9, 1927, 31

Parable for a Certain Virgin
(*Gun, Well*)   New Yorker, Apr 23, 1927, 27

A Pig's-Eye View of Literature (PEVL):
Oscar Wilde (*Gun, Well*)   Life, Jun 2, 1927, 13

PEVL: The Lives and Times of John Keats,
Percy Bysshe Shelley, and George Gordon,
Lord Byron (*Gun, Well*)   Life, Jun 2, 1927, 13

PEVL: Walter Savage Landor (*Gun, Well*)   Life, Jun 2, 1927, 13

PEVL: Harriet Beecher Stowe (*Gun, Well*)   Life, Jun 2, 1927, 13

PEVL: Alfred Lord Tennyson (*Gun, Well*)   Life, Jun 2, 1927, 13

PEVL: D. G. Rossetti (*Gun, Well*)   Life, Jun 2, 1927, 13

PEVL: George Sand (*Gun, Well*)   Life, Jun 2, 1927, 13

PEVL: George Gissing (*Gun, Well*)   Life, Jun 2, 1927, 13

PEVL: Thomas Carlyle (*Gun, Well*)   Life, Jun 2, 1927, 13

PEVL: Alfred Dumas and His Son (*Gun, Well*)	*Life,* Jun 2, 1927, 13
PEVL: Charles Dickens (*Gun, Well*)	*Life,* Jun 2, 1927, 13
The Red Dress (*Gun, Well*)	*Life,* Jun 9, 1927, 13
To a Lady, Who Must Write Verse [For a Lady Who Must Write Verse] (*Gun, Well*)	*New Yorker,* Jun 18, 1927, 22
Daylight Saving (*Gun, Well*)	*New Yorker,* Jul 2, 1927, 26
Story (*Gun, Well*)	*Life,* Jul 14, 1927, 15
Pour Prendre Congé (*Gun, Well*)	*New Yorker,* Jul 16, 1927, 21
Frustration (*Gun, Well*)	*New Yorker,* Jul 23, 1927, 25
The Counsellor [The Counselor; to Newcastle] (*Gun, Well*)	*Life,* Jul 28, 1927, 13
The Homebody (*Gun, Well*)	*New Republic,* Aug 3, 1927, 282
Godmother (*Gun, Well*)	NY *World,* Aug 23, 1927, 13
Bric-A-Brac (*Gun, Well*)	*Bookman,* Sep 1927, 33
Bohemia (*Gun, Well*)	*New Yorker,* Sep 17, 1927, 25
Landscape (*Gun, Well*)	*Bookman,* Nov 1927, 271
Songs for the Nearest Harmonica (SFNH): Fairy Story [Fable] (*Gun, Well*)	*New Yorker,* Nov 12, 1927, 28
SFNH: But Not Forgotten (*Gun, Well*)	*New Yorker,* Nov 12, 1927, 28
SFNH: Reuben's Children (*Gun, Well*)	*New Yorker,* Nov 12, 1927, 28
SFNH: Incurable (*Gun, Well*)	*New Yorker,* Nov 12, 1927, 28
Chris-Cross (*Fun*)	*New Yorker,* Nov 12, 1927, 112 *[4]
Interior (*Gun, Well*)	*Nation,* Nov 30, 1927, 598
The Maid-Servant at the Inn (*Gun, Well*)	*Bookman,* Dec 1927, 340

The Gentlest Lady (*Gun, Well*)	*McCall's*, Dec 1927, 17
SFNH: Wisdom (*Gun, Well*)	*New Yorker*, Jan 7, 1928, 21
SFNH: For R. C. B. (*Gun, Well*)	*New Yorker*, Jan 7, 1928, 21
SFNH: Penelope (*Gun, Well*)	*New Yorker*, Jan 7, 1928, 21
SFNH: Surprise (*Gun, Well*)	*New Yorker*, Jan 7, 1928, 21
SFNH: Post-Graduate (*Gun, Well*)	*New Yorker*, Jan 7, 1928, 21
Fair Weather (*Gun, Well*)	NY *World*, Jan 20, 1928, 13
The Whistling Girl (*Gun, Well*)	NY *World*, Mar 15, 1928, 13
The Last Question (*Gun, Well*)	NY *World*, Mar 20, 1928, 13
Coda (*Gun, Well*)	NY *World*, Mar 22, 1928, 13
SFNH: The Searched Soul (*Gun, Well*)	*New Yorker*, May 26, 1928, 20
SFNH: Solace (*Taxes, Well*)	*New Yorker*, May 26, 1928, 20
SFNH: On Cheating the Fiddler (*Gun, Well*)	*New Yorker*, May 26, 1928, 20
SFNH: Rhyme Against Living (*Gun, Well*)	*New Yorker*, May 26, 1928, 20
SFNH: Distance (*Taxes, Well*)	*New Yorker*, May 26, 1928, 20
SFNH: Grande Passion (*Fun*)	*New Yorker*, May 26, 1928, 20
Excursion Into Assonance (*Fun*)	NY *World*, Aug 17, 1928, 11
—And Return (*Fun*)	NY *World*, Aug 17, 1928, 11
Garden-Spot (*Taxes, Well*)	NY *World*, Sep 4, 1928, 11
Prayer for a New Mother (*Taxes, Well*)	*Bookman*, Dec 1928, 376
Song of Social Life in Hollywood (*Fun*)	NY *World*, Dec 12, 1928, 15

Purposely Ungrammatical Love Song
(*Taxes, Well*)   NY *World,* Dec 25, 1928, 15

Midnight (*Taxes, Well*)   NY *World,* Jan 14, 1929, 11

The Danger of Writing Defiant
Verse (*Taxes, Well*)   NY *World,* Mar 15, 1929, 15

Tombstones in the Starlight (TIS):
The Minor Poet (*Taxes, Well*)   *New Yorker,* May 4, 1929, 22

TIS: The Pretty Lady (*Taxes, Well*)   *New Yorker,* May 4, 1929, 22

TIS: The Very Rich Man (*Taxes, Well*)   *New Yorker,* May 4, 1929, 22

TIS: The Fisherwoman (*Taxes, Well*)   *New Yorker,* May 4, 1929, 22

TIS: The Crusader (*Taxes, Well*)   *New Yorker,* May 4, 1929, 22

TIS: The Actress (*Taxes, Well*)   *New Yorker,* May 4, 1929, 22

Sonnet [2] (*Fun*)   NY *World,* Aug 16, 1929, 11

If It Be Not Fair— [Ultimatum]
(*Taxes, Well*)   *New Yorker,* Aug 24, 1929, 14

The Evening Primrose (*Taxes, Well*)   *New Yorker,* Aug 24, 1929, 14

Little Words (*Taxes, Well*)   *New Yorker,* Aug 24, 1929, 14

Sonnet on an Alpine Mount [Sonnet
on an Alpine Night] (*Taxes, Well*)   NY *World,* Nov 19, 1929, 13

The Beloved Ladies (TBL): Salome's
Dancing-Lesson (*Taxes, Well*)   *New Yorker,* Dec 14, 1929, 27

TBL: Ninon De L'enclos, on Her
Last Birthday (*Taxes, Well*)   *New Yorker,* Dec 14, 1929, 27

TBL: Guinevere at Her Fireside
(*Taxes, Well*)   *New Yorker,* Dec 14, 1929, 27

TBL: From a Letter From Lesbia
(*Taxes, Well*)   *New Yorker,* Dec 14, 1929, 27

Prayer for a Prayer (*Taxes, Well*)	NY *World*, Apr 28, 1930, 13
Vers Démodé (*Taxes, Well*)	NY *World*, Apr 29, 1930, 13
A Cup of Coffee, a Sandwich, and Yew (CCSY): Prologue to a Saga (*Taxes, Well*)	NY *World*, Jun 25, 1930, 11
CCSY: Ornithology for Beginners (*Taxes, Well*)	NY *World*, Jun 25, 1930, 11
CCSY: Lines on Reading Too Much Verse [Lines on Reading Too Many Poets] (*Taxes, Well*)	NY *World*, Jun 25, 1930, 11
CCSY: The Apple Tree (*Taxes, Well*)	NY *World*, Jun 25, 1930, 11
CCSY: Requiescat (*Taxes, Well*)	NY *World*, Jun 25, 1930, 11
The Little Old Lady in Lavender Silk (*Taxes, Well*)	NY *World*, Aug 1, 1930, 11
Take My Vows [Sonnet for the End of a Sequence] (*Taxes, Well*)	*Yale Review*, Sep 1930, 139
For a Woman, Dead Young [Of a Woman, Dead Young] (*Taxes, Well*)	NY *World*, Sep 15, 1930, 11
Ballade of Unfortunate Mammals (*Taxes, Well*)	NY *World*, Jan 8, 1931, 13
Letter to Ogden Nash (*Fun*)	*Saturday Review*, Jan 17, 1931, 544
After a Spanish Proverb (*Taxes, Well*)	NY *Herald Tribune*, Mar 3, 1931, 26
Ballade of a Talked-Off Ear (*Taxes, Well*)	NY *Herald Tribune*, Mar 26, 1931, 20
My Own (*Taxes, Well*)	NY *Herald Tribune*, Apr 21, 1931, 30
The Sea (*Taxes, Well*)	NY *Herald Tribune*, Apr 30, 1931, 20

Pastoraliana (P): Sweet Violets
(*Taxes, Well*)   NY *Herald Tribune,* May 7, 1931, 20

P: Cherry White (*Taxes, Well*)   NY *Herald Tribune,* May 7, 1931, 20

P: Sanctuary (*Taxes, Well*)   NY *Herald Tribune,* May 7, 1931, 20

P: In the Meadow (*Taxes* only)   NY *Herald Tribune,* May 7, 1931, 20

P: The Willow (*Taxes, Well*)   NY *Herald Tribune,* May 7, 1931, 20

After Dawn (*Fun*)   *New Yorker,* May 30, 1931, 66 *[4]

Song in the Worst
Possible Taste (*Fun*)   NY *Herald Tribune,* Oct 15, 1931, 21

Sight (*Well* only)   NY *Herald Tribune,* Apr 21, 1932, 15

Our Cousins (*Fun*)   NY *Herald Tribune,* Dec 3, 1932, 11

The Lady's Reward
(*Well* only)   NY *Herald Tribune,* Apr 13, 1933, 15

Prisoner (*Well* only)   NY *Herald Tribune,* Oct 23, 1933, 13

Autumn Valentine
(*Well* only)   NY *Herald Tribune,* Nov 7, 1935, 21

Blurb (*Fun 2* only)   Unpublished, Sep 18, 1936[†]

The Passionate Screen Writer
to His Love (*Fun,* in full *Fun 2* only)   Unpublished, 1937[‡]

Threat to a Fickle Lady (*Fun*)   *New Yorker,* Mar 26, 1938, 20

Pecking Order (or "Eggs Tempore")
(*Fun 2* only)   Unpublished, Jan–Mar 1941[§]

War Song (*Portable* only)   *New Yorker,* Mar 4, 1944, 22

Free Verse	Source, Date, Page
Women: A Hate Song (*Fun*)	*Vanity Fair,* Aug 1916, 61*[2]
Men: A Hate Song (*Fun*)	*Vanity Fair,* Feb 1917, 65*[1]
Actresses: A Hate Song (*Fun*)	*Vanity Fair,* May 1917, 64*[1]
Relatives: A Hate Song (*Fun*)	*Vanity Fair,* Aug 1917, 39*[1]
Slackers: A Hate Song (*Fun*)	*Vanity Fair,* Dec 1917, 83
Bohemians: A Hate Song (*Fun*)	*Vanity Fair,* Oct 1918, 46
Our Office: A Hate Song (*Fun*)	*Vanity Fair,* May 1919, 6
Actors: A Hate Song (*Fun*)	*Vanity Fair,* Jul 1919, 37
A Hymn of Hate: Bores (*Fun*)	*Life,* Nov 18, 1920, 902
A Hymn of Hate: The Drama (*Fun*)	*Life,* May 5, 1921, 636
A Hymn of Hate: Parties (*Fun*)	*Life,* Jun 2, 1921, 790
A Hymn of Hate: Movies (*Fun*)	*Life,* Jul 21, 1921, 10
A Hymn of Hate: Books (*Fun*)	*Life,* Dec 22, 1921, 12
A Hymn of Hate: The Younger Set (*Fun*)	*Life,* Mar 30, 1922, 8
A Hymn of Hate: Summer Resorts (*Fun*)	*Life,* Aug 17, 1922, 10
A Hymn of Hate: Reformers (*Fun 2* only)	*Nonsenseorship,* 1922, 95°
A Hymn of Hate: Wives (*Fun*)	*Life,* May 10, 1923, 8
A Hymn of Hate: Husbands (*Fun*)	*Life,* Nov 15, 1923, 8
A Hymn of Hate: College Boys (*Fun*)	*Life,* Nov 13, 1924, 12

Previously Collected Poems Without Earlier Citations

Anecdote (*Rope, Well*)

Ballade of a Great Weariness (*Rope, Well*)¶

The Dramatists (*Rope, Well*)¶

The False Friends (*Rope, Well*)¶

For a Sad Lady (*Rope, Well*)

Pattern (*Rope, Well*)

Spring Song (*Rope* only)

They Part (*Rope, Well*)

The Veteran (*Rope, Well*)

Dilemma (*Gun, Well*)

Directions for Finding the Bard (*Gun* only)

Liebestod (*Gun, Well*)

Second Love (*Gun, Well*)

Victoria (*Gun, Well*)

The Flaw in Paganism (*Taxes, Well*)

Iseult of Brittany (*Taxes, Well*)

"Star Light, Star Bright—" (*Taxes, Well*)

Transition (*Taxes, Well*)

Summary (*Taxes, Well*)

Temps Perdu (*Well* only)

* First published pseudonymously (under a name other than "Dorothy Parker" or the initials "D. P.") or anonymously: "Dorothy Rothschild" (her birth name) [*¹]; "Henriette Rousseau" [*²]; "Helen Wells" [*³]; "Constant Reader" [*⁴]; or anonymous [*⁵].

† The date listed here is taken from the postmark on the postcard that Dorothy Parker sent from her "Fox House" near Doylestown, Pennsylvania, to "Mr. Marshall A. Best, The Viking Press Inc., 18 East 48th Street, New York City." The postcard text: "You may quote this rhymed review of F.P.A's new book: 'An instrument that is far from rifty / Is "The Melancholy Lute." (2.50).' . . . If that isn't the price of the book, I'll do another at once." The rhyme appeared on the dust jacket of Franklin P. Adams's *The Melancholy Lute,* published 1936. The editor thanks Kevin Fitzpatrick for bringing it to his attention, and Anthony Adams and the estate of Franklin P. Adams for supplying the image of the postcard containing the original draft of the text. The version that appears in the text is taken from the dust jacket.

‡ The date listed here is supplied by Marion Meade in *Dorothy Parker: What Fresh Hell Is This?* (1987), which reproduced the first eight lines (of the thirty-two in the full text) and stated: "Marc Connelly carefully preserved it among his papers." (at 277, 433). It evidently first appeared in print in Kenneth Macgowan's *Behind the Screen: The History and Techniques of the Motion Picture* (1965) (at 379). Macgowan credited its first publication to the *Screen Writer,* a periodical published by the Screen Writers Guild during the late 1940s, but an examination of archived issues did not find it. Only those first eight lines appeared in the first edition of *Not Much Fun*; the full text appears in this edition.

§ Dorothy Parker dashed this off after Somerset Maugham challenged her to write a poem at a Los Angeles dinner party (see footnote 81, pages 48–49). The date listed here is deduced from information supplied by Ted Morgan in *Maugham* (1980): (1) "In January [1941] he [Maugham] went to San Francisco. . . . His next stop was Los Angeles." (2) "He was seated next to Dorothy Parker. . . . 'Why don't you write a poem for me?' Maugham asked." And (3) "Maugham left Los Angeles in early March" (at 452–54). Conclusion: the dinner party occurred between January and early March 1941. The item first appeared in print in Maugham's introduction to the *Portable Dorothy Parker* (at 13), published in 1944.

° *Nonsenseorship* is a collection of "sundry observations concerning prohibitions, inhibitions, and illegalities" supplied by fifteen contributors that included the Algonquin Round Table regulars Dorothy Parker, Heywood Broun, Ruth Hale, and Alexander Woollcott, and also Ben Hecht. It was illustrated by Ralph Barton and published in New York by G. P. Putnam's Sons in 1922.

¶ Appeared in *Life* magazine 1927–30; that is, *after* being collected in *Enough Rope,* published in 1926. Therefore, *Enough Rope*—not *Life* magazine—is the first known publication source.

Upon hearing of the poet George Crabbe's death in 1832, the British home secretary (and later prime minister) Lord Melbourne declared, "I am always glad when one of these fellows dies, for then I know I have the whole of him on my shelf."

Permissions and Acknowledgments

Grateful acknowledgment is given to the following:

The Publisher and Mr. Silverstein wish to thank the National Association for the Advancement of Colored People for authorizing the use of Dorothy Parker's works.

"Letter to Robert Benchley" courtesy of the Department of Special Collections, Mugar Memorial Library, Boston University.

"Ballade of Understandable Ambitions" reprinted from the *Saturday Evening Post* © 1923, 1950; "Song of a Contented Heart" reprinted from the *Saturday Evening Post* © 1923, 1950; "Song of the Wilderness" reprinted from the *Saturday Evening Post* © 1923, 1950; "A Triolet" reprinted from the *Saturday Evening Post* © 1923, 1950; "Pæan" reprinted from the *Saturday Evening Post* © 1923, 1950; "Song [3]" reprinted from the *Saturday Evening Post* © 1923, 1950; "And Oblige" reprinted from the *Saturday Evening Post* © 1923, 1950; "Triolet [2]" reprinted from the *Saturday Evening Post* © 1923, 1950.

The verses "Christopher Morley goes hippetty, hoppetty . . ." ["Chris-Cross"] and "Theodore Dreiser should ought to write nicer" ["After Dawn"] originally appeared in the *New Yorker* under the rubric "Reading and Writing" by Dorothy Parker © 1927, 1931, 1958, 1959 The New Yorker Magazine, Inc. (formerly The F-R Publishing Corp.)

The verse "An instrument that is far from rifty . . ." ["Blurb"] is supplied courtesy of Anthony Adams and the estate of Franklin P. Adams.

"Pollyanna Gets the Air," typeset image courtesy of the Fales Manuscripts Collection, Box 136, Folder 10, Fales Library, New York University.

Mr. Silverstein also wishes to extend particular thanks to Laura Ruttum and Thomas Lannon, Manuscripts and Archives Division, New York Public Library; Lisa Darms and Marvin J. Taylor, Fales Library and Special Collections, New York University; Kevin Fitzpatrick; Peter Lampack; Gillian Blake; and Whitney Frick.